THE ODYSSEY

Homer

SPARK PUBLISHING

© 2002, 2007 by Spark Publishing, A Division of Barnes & Noble

This Spark Publishing edition 2014 by SparkNotes LLC, an Affiliate of Barnes & Noble

122 Fifth Avenue
New York, NY 10011
www.sparknotes.com

ISBN 978-1-4114-6976-1

Please submit changes or report errors to www.sparknotes.com/errors.

Printed in Canada

10 9 8 7 6 5 4

CONTENTS

CONTEXT

NEARLY THREE THOUSAND YEARS after they were composed, *The Iliad* and *The Odyssey* remain two of the most celebrated and widely read stories ever told, yet next to nothing is known about their author. He was certainly an accomplished Greek bard, and he probably lived in the late eighth and early seventh centuries B.C.E. Authorship is traditionally ascribed to a blind poet named Homer, and it is under this name that the works are still published. Greeks of the third and second centuries B.C.E., however, already questioned whether Homer existed and whether the two epics were even written by a single individual.

Most modern scholars believe that even if a single person wrote the epics, his work owed a tremendous debt to a long tradition of unwritten, oral poetry. Stories of a glorious expedition to the East and of its leaders' fateful journeys home had been circulating in Greece for hundreds of years before *The Iliad* and *The Odyssey* were composed. Casual storytellers and semiprofessional minstrels passed these stories down through generations, with each artist developing and polishing the story as he told it. According to this theory, one poet, multiple poets working in collaboration, or perhaps even a series of poets handing down their work in succession finally turned these stories into written works, again with each adding his own touch and expanding or contracting certain episodes in the overall narrative to fit his taste.

Although historical, archaeological, and linguistic evidence suggests that the epics were composed between 750 and 650 B.C.E., they are set in Mycenaean Greece in about the twelfth century B.C.E., during the Bronze Age. This earlier period, the Greeks believed, was a more glorious and sublime age, when gods still frequented the earth and heroic, godlike mortals with superhuman attributes populated Greece. Because the two epics strive to evoke this pristine age, they are written in a high style and generally depict life as it was believed to have been led in the great kingdoms of the Bronze Age. The Greeks are often referred to as "Achaeans," the name of a large tribe occupying Greece during the Bronze Age.

But Homer's reconstruction often yields to the realities of eighth- and seventh-century B.C.E. Greece. The feudal social structure apparent in the background of *The Odyssey* seems more akin to Homer's Greece than to Odysseus's, and Homer substitutes the pantheon of deities of his own day for the related but different gods whom Mycenaean Greeks worshipped. Many other minor but obvious anachronisms—such as references to iron tools and to tribes that had not yet migrated to Greece by the Bronze Age—betray the poem's later, Iron Age origins.

Of the two epics, *The Odyssey* is the later both in setting and, probably, date of composition. *The Iliad* tells the story of the Greek struggle to rescue Helen, a Greek queen, from her Trojan captors. *The Odyssey* takes the fall of the city of Troy as its starting point and crafts a new epic around the struggle of one of those Greek warriors, the hero Odysseus. It tells the story of his *nostos,* or journey home, to northwest Greece during the ten-year period after the Greek victory over the Trojans. A tale of wandering, it takes place not on a field of battle but on fantastic islands and foreign lands. After the unrelenting tragedy and carnage of *The Iliad, The Odyssey* often strikes readers as comic or surreal at times. This quality has led some scholars to conclude that Homer wrote *The Odyssey* at a later time of his life, when he showed less interest in struggles at arms and was more receptive to a storyline that focused on the fortunes and misadventures of a single man. Others argue that someone else must have composed *The Odyssey,* one who wished to provide a companion work to *The Iliad* but had different interests from those of the earlier epic's author.

Like *The Iliad, The Odyssey* was composed primarily in the Ionic dialect of Ancient Greek, which was spoken on the Aegean islands and in the coastal settlements of Asia Minor, now modern Turkey. Some scholars thus conclude that the poet hailed from somewhere in the eastern Greek world. More likely, however, the poet chose the Ionic dialect because he felt it to be more appropriate for the high style and grand scope of his work. Slightly later Greek literature suggests that poets varied the dialects of their poems according to the themes that they were treating and might write in dialects that they didn't actually speak. Homer's epics, moreover, are Panhellenic (encompassing all of Greece) in spirit and, in fact, use forms from several other dialects, suggesting that Homer didn't simply fall back on his native tongue but rather suited his poems to the dialect that would best complement his ideas.

PLOT OVERVIEW

TEN YEARS HAVE PASSED since the fall of Troy, and the Greek hero Odysseus still has not returned to his kingdom in Ithaca. A large and rowdy mob of suitors who have overrun Odysseus's palace and pillaged his land continue to court his wife, Penelope. She has remained faithful to Odysseus. Prince Telemachus, Odysseus's son, wants desperately to throw them out but does not have the confidence or experience to fight them. One of the suitors, Antinous, plans to assassinate the young prince, eliminating the only opposition to their dominion over the palace.

Unknown to the suitors, Odysseus is still alive. The beautiful nymph Calypso, possessed by love for him, has imprisoned him on her island, Ogygia. He longs to return to his wife and son, but he has no ship or crew to help him escape. While the gods and goddesses of Mount Olympus debate Odysseus's future, Athena, Odysseus's strongest supporter among the gods, resolves to help Telemachus. Disguised as a friend of the prince's grandfather, Laertes, she convinces the prince to call a meeting of the assembly at which he reproaches the suitors. Athena also prepares him for a great journey to Pylos and Sparta, where the kings Nestor and Menelaus, Odysseus's companions during the war, inform him that Odysseus is alive and trapped on Calypso's island. Telemachus makes plans to return home, while, back in Ithaca, Antinous and the other suitors prepare an ambush to kill him when he reaches port.

On Mount Olympus, Zeus sends Hermes to rescue Odysseus from Calypso. Hermes persuades Calypso to let Odysseus build a ship and leave. The homesick hero sets sail, but when Poseidon, god of the sea, finds him sailing home, he sends a storm to wreck Odysseus's ship. Poseidon has harbored a bitter grudge against Odysseus since the hero blinded his son, the Cyclops Polyphemus, earlier in his travels. Athena intervenes to save Odysseus from Poseidon's wrath, and the beleaguered king lands at Scheria, home of the Phaeacians. Nausicaa, the Phaeacian princess, shows him to the royal palace, and Odysseus receives a warm welcome from the king and queen. When he identifies himself as Odysseus, his hosts, who have heard of his exploits at Troy, are stunned. They promise to give him safe passage to Ithaca, but first they beg to hear the story of his adventures.

Odysseus spends the night describing the fantastic chain of events leading up to his arrival on Calypso's island. He recounts his trip to the Land of the Lotus Eaters, his battle with Polyphemus the Cyclops, his love affair with the witch-goddess Circe, his temptation by the deadly Sirens, his journey into Hades to consult the prophet Tiresias, and his fight with the sea monster Scylla. When he finishes his story, the Phaeacians return Odysseus to Ithaca, where he seeks out the hut of his faithful swineherd, Eumaeus. Though Athena has disguised Odysseus as a beggar, Eumaeus warmly receives and nourishes him in the hut. He soon encounters Telemachus, who has returned from Pylos and Sparta despite the suitors' ambush, and reveals to him his true identity. Odysseus and Telemachus devise a plan to massacre the suitors and regain control of Ithaca.

When Odysseus arrives at the palace the next day, still disguised as a beggar, he endures abuse and insults from the suitors. The only person who recognizes him is his old nurse, Eurycleia, but she swears not to disclose his secret. Penelope takes an interest in this strange beggar, suspecting that he might be her long-lost husband. Quite crafty herself, Penelope organizes an archery contest the following day and promises to marry any man who can string Odysseus's great bow and fire an arrow through a row of twelve axes—a feat that only Odysseus has ever been able to accomplish. At the contest, each suitor tries to string the bow and fails. Odysseus steps up to the bow and, with little effort, fires an arrow through all twelve axes. He then turns the bow on the suitors. He and Telemachus, assisted by a few faithful servants, kill every last suitor.

Odysseus reveals himself to the entire palace and reunites with his loving Penelope. He travels to the outskirts of Ithaca to see his aging father, Laertes. They come under attack from the vengeful family members of the dead suitors, but Laertes, reinvigorated by his son's return, successfully kills Antinous's father and puts a stop to the attack. Zeus dispatches Athena to restore peace. With his power secure and his family reunited, Odysseus's long ordeal comes to an end.

Character List

Odysseus The protagonist of *The Odyssey*. Odysseus fought among the other Greek heroes at Troy and now struggles to return to his kingdom in Ithaca. Odysseus is the husband of Queen Penelope and the father of Prince Telemachus. Though a strong and courageous warrior, he is most renowned for his cunning. He is a favorite of the goddess Athena, who often sends him divine aid, but a bitter enemy of Poseidon, who frustrates his journey at every turn.

Telemachus Odysseus's son. An infant when Odysseus left for Troy, Telemachus is about twenty at the beginning of the story. He is a natural obstacle to the suitors desperately courting his mother, but despite his courage and good heart, he initially lacks the poise and confidence to oppose them. His maturation, especially during his trip to Pylos and Sparta in Books 3 and 4, provides a subplot to the epic. Athena often assists him.

Penelope Wife of Odysseus and mother of Telemachus. Penelope spends her days in the palace pining for the husband who left for Troy twenty years earlier and never returned. Homer portrays her as sometimes flighty and excitable but also clever and steadfastly true to her husband.

Athena Daughter of Zeus and goddess of wisdom, purposeful battle, and the womanly arts. Athena assists Odysseus and Telemachus with divine powers throughout the epic, and she speaks up for them in the councils of the gods on Mount Olympus. She often appears in disguise as Mentor, an old friend of Odysseus.

Poseidon God of the sea. As the suitors are Odysseus's mortal antagonists, Poseidon is his divine antagonist. He despises Odysseus for blinding his son, the Cyclops Polyphemus, and constantly hampers his journey home. Ironically, Poseidon is the patron of the seafaring Phaeacians, who ultimately help to return Odysseus to Ithaca.

Zeus   King of gods and men, who mediates the disputes of the gods on Mount Olympus. Zeus is occasionally depicted as weighing men's fates in his scales. He sometimes helps Odysseus or permits Athena to do the same.

Antinous   The most arrogant of Penelope's suitors. Antinous leads the campaign to have Telemachus killed. Unlike the other suitors, he is never portrayed sympathetically, and he is the first to die when Odysseus returns.

Eurymachus   A manipulative, deceitful suitor. Eurymachus's charisma and duplicity allow him to exert some influence over the other suitors.

Amphinomus   Among the dozens of suitors, the only decent man seeking Penelope's hand in marriage. Amphinomus sometimes speaks up for Odysseus and Telemachus, but he is killed like the rest of the suitors in the final fight.

Eumaeus   The loyal shepherd who, along with the cowherd Philoetius, helps Odysseus reclaim his throne after his return to Ithaca. Even though he does not know that the vagabond who appears at his hut is Odysseus, Eumaeus gives the man food and shelter.

Eurycleia   The aged and loyal servant who nursed Odysseus and Telemachus when they were babies. Eurycleia is well informed about palace intrigues and serves as confidante to her masters. She keeps Telemachus's journey secret from Penelope, and she later keeps Odysseus's identity a secret after she recognizes a scar on his leg.

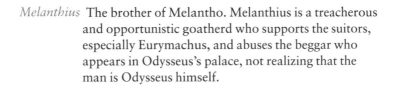

Melanthius The brother of Melantho. Melanthius is a treacherous and opportunistic goatherd who supports the suitors, especially Eurymachus, and abuses the beggar who appears in Odysseus's palace, not realizing that the man is Odysseus himself.

Melantho Sister of Melanthius and maidservant in Odysseus's palace. Like her brother, Melantho abuses the beggar in the palace, not knowing that the man is Odysseus. She is having an affair with Eurymachus.

Calypso The beautiful nymph who falls in love with Odysseus when he lands on her island-home of Ogygia. Calypso holds him prisoner there for seven years until Hermes, the messenger god, persuades her to let him go.

Polyphemus One of the Cyclopes (uncivilized one-eyed giants) whose island Odysseus comes to soon after leaving Troy. Polyphemus imprisons Odysseus and his crew and tries to eat them, but Odysseus blinds him through a clever ruse and manages to escape. In doing so, however, Odysseus angers Polyphemus's father, Poseidon.

Circe The beautiful witch-goddess who transforms Odysseus's crew into swine when he lands on her island. With Hermes' help, Odysseus resists Circe's powers and then becomes her lover, living in luxury at her side for a year.

Laertes Odysseus's aging father, who resides on a farm in Ithaca. In despair and physical decline, Laertes regains his spirit when Odysseus returns and eventually kills Antinous's father.

Tiresias A Theban prophet who inhabits the underworld. Tiresias meets Odysseus when Odysseus journeys to the underworld in Book 11. He shows Odysseus how to get back to Ithaca and allows Odysseus to communicate with the other souls in Hades.

Nestor   King of Pylos and a former warrior in the Trojan War. Like Odysseus, Nestor is known as a clever speaker. Telemachus visits him in Book 3 to ask about his father, but Nestor knows little of Odysseus's whereabouts.

Menelaus   King of Sparta, brother of Agamemnon, and husband of Helen, he helped lead the Greeks in the Trojan War. He offers Telemachus assistance in his quest to find Odysseus when Telemachus visits him in Book 4.

Helen   Wife of Menelaus and queen of Sparta. Helen's abduction from Sparta by the Trojans sparked the Trojan War. Her beauty is without parallel, but she is criticized for giving in to her Trojan captors and thereby costing many Greek men their lives. She offers Telemachus assistance in his quest to find his father.

Agamemnon   Former king of Mycenae, brother of Menelaus, and commander of the Achaean forces at Troy. Odysseus encounters Agamemnon's spirit in Hades. Agamemnon was murdered by his wife, Clytemnestra, and her lover, Aegisthus, upon his return from the war. He was later avenged by his son Orestes. Their story is constantly repeated in *The Odyssey* to offer an inverted image of the fortunes of Odysseus and Telemachus.

Nausicaa   The beautiful daughter of King Alcinous and Queen Arete of the Phaeacians. Nausicaa discovers Odysseus on the beach at Scheria and, out of budding affection for him, ensures his warm reception at her parents' palace.

Alcinous   King of the Phaeacians, who offers Odysseus hospitality in his island kingdom of Scheria. Alcinous hears the story of Odysseus's wanderings and provides him with safe passage back to Ithaca.

Arete   Queen of the Phaeacians, wife of Alcinous, and mother of Nausicaa. Arete is intelligent and influential. Nausicaa tells Odysseus to make his appeal for assistance to Arete.

ANALYSIS OF MAJOR CHARACTERS

ODYSSEUS

Odysseus has the defining character traits of a Homeric leader: strength, courage, nobility, a thirst for glory, and confidence in his authority. His most distinguishing trait, however, is his sharp intellect. Odysseus's quick thinking helps him out of some very tough situations, as when he escapes from the cave of the Cyclops in Book 9, or when he hides his slaughter of the suitors by having his minstrel strike up a wedding tune in Book 23. He is also a convincing, articulate speaker and can win over or manipulate his audience with ease. When he first addresses Nausicaa on the island of Scheria, for example, his suave, comforting approach quickly wins her trust.

Like other Homeric heroes, Odysseus longs to win *kleos* ("glory" won through great deeds), but he also wishes to complete his *nostos* ("homecoming"). He enjoys his luxurious life with Calypso in an exotic land, but only to a point. Eventually, he wants to return home, even though he admits that his wife cannot compare with Calypso. He thinks of home throughout the time he spends with the Phaeacians and also while on Circe's island. Sometimes his glory-seeking gets in the way of his home-seeking, however. He sacks the land of the Cicones but loses men and time in the process. He waits too long in the cave of Polyphemus, enjoying the free milk and cheese he finds, and is trapped there when the Cyclops returns.

Homeric characters are generally static. Though they may be very complex and realistic, they do not change over the course of the work as characters in modern novels and stories do. Odysseus and especially Telemachus break this rule. Early in his adventures, Odysseus's love of glory prompts him to reveal his identity to the Cyclops and bring Poseidon's wrath down on him. By the end of the epic, he seems much more willing to temper pride with patience. Disguised as a beggar, he does not immediately react to the abuse he receives from the suitors. Instead, he endures it until the traps he has set and the loyalties he has secured put him in a position from which he can strike back effectively.

TELEMACHUS

Just an infant when his father left for Troy, Telemachus is still matur-
ing when *The Odyssey* begins. He is wholly devoted to his mother
and to maintaining his father's estate, but he does not know how
to protect them from the suitors. After all, it has only been a few
years since he first realized what the suitors' intentions were. His
meeting with Athena in Book 1 changes things. Aside from improv-
ing his stature and bearing, she teaches him the responsibilities of
a young prince. He soon becomes more assertive. He confronts the
suitors and denounces the abuse of his estate, and when Penelope
and Eurycleia become anxious or upset, he does not shy away from
taking control.

Telemachus never fully matches his father's talents, at least not by
The Odyssey's conclusion. He has a stout heart and an active mind,
and sometimes even a bit of a temper, but he never schemes with
the same skill or speaks with quite the same fluency as Odysseus.
In Book 22, he accidentally leaves a weapons storeroom unlocked,
a careless mistake that allows the suitors to arm themselves. While
Odysseus does make a few mistakes in judgment over the course
of the epic, it is difficult to imagine him making such an absent-
minded blunder. Telemachus has not yet inherited his father's brassy
pride either. The scene with the bow captures the endpoint of his
development perfectly. He tries and tries to string it, and very nearly
does, but not quite. This episode reminds us that, at the close of *The
Odyssey*, Telemachus still cannot match his father's skills but is well
on his way.

PENELOPE

Though she has not seen Odysseus in twenty years, and despite pres-
sure the suitors place on her to remarry, Penelope never loses faith
in her husband. Her cares make her somewhat flighty and excitable,
however. For this reason, Odysseus, Telemachus, and Athena often
prefer to leave her in the dark about matters rather than upset her.
Athena must distract her, for instance, so that she does not discover
Odysseus's identity when Eurycleia is washing him. Athena often
comes to her in dreams to reassure or comfort her, for Penelope
would otherwise spend her nights weeping in her bed.

Though her love for Odysseus is unyielding, she responds to the
suitors with some indecision. She never refuses to remarry outright.

Instead, she puts off her decision and leads them on with promises that she will choose a new husband as soon as certain things happen. Her astute delaying tactics reveal her sly and artful side. The notion of not remarrying until she completes a burial shroud that she will never complete cleverly buys her time. Similarly, some commentators claim that her decision to marry whomever wins the archery contest of Book 21 results from her awareness that only her husband can win it. Some even claim that she recognizes her husband before she admits it to him in Book 23.

ATHENA

As goddess of wisdom and battle, Athena naturally has a soft spot for the brave and wily Odysseus. She helps him out of many tough situations, including his shipwreck in Book 5 and the mismatched battle of Book 22. She does not merely impart sense and safety to her passive charge, however. She takes an interest in Odysseus for the talents he already has and actively demonstrates. Although she reassures Odysseus during the battle with the suitors, she does not become fully involved, preferring instead to watch Odysseus fight and prevail on his own.

She also often helps Telemachus—as when she sends him off to Pylos and Sparta to earn a name for himself—but she has the most affection for Odysseus. Athena is confident, practical, clever, a master of disguises, and a great warrior, characteristics she finds reflected in Telemachus. Her role as goddess of the womanly arts gets very little attention in *The Odyssey*. Penelope works at the loom all the time but rarely sees Athena, and then usually only in dreams.

Themes, Motifs & Symbols

Themes

The Power of Cunning over Strength

If *The Iliad* is about strength, *The Odyssey* is about cunning, a difference that becomes apparent in the very first lines of the epics. Whereas *The Iliad* tells the story of the rage of Achilles, the strongest hero in the Greek army, *The Odyssey* focuses on a "man of twists and turns" (1.1). Odysseus does have extraordinary strength, as he demonstrates in Book 21 by being the only man who can string the bow. But he relies much more on mind than muscle, a tendency that his encounters showcase. He knows that he cannot overpower Polyphemus, for example, and that, even if he were able to do so, he wouldn't be able to budge the boulder from the door. He thus schemes around his disadvantage in strength by exploiting Polyphemus's stupidity. Though he does use violence to put out Polyphemus's single eye, this display of strength is part of a larger plan to deceive the brute.

Similarly, Odysseus knows that he is no match for the host of strapping young suitors in his palace, so he makes the most of his other strength—his wits. Step by step, through disguises and deceptions, he arranges a situation in which he alone is armed and the suitors are locked in a room with him. With this setup, Achilles' superb talents as a warrior would enable him to accomplish what Odysseus does, but only Odysseus's strategic planning can bring about such a sure victory. Some of the tests in Odysseus's long, wandering ordeal seem to mock reliance on strength alone. No one can resist the Sirens' song, for example, but Odysseus gets an earful of the lovely melody by having his crew tie him up. Scylla and Charybdis cannot be beaten, but Odysseus can minimize his losses with prudent decision-making and careful navigation. Odysseus's encounter with Achilles in the underworld is a reminder: Achilles won great *kleos*, or glory, during his life, but that life was brief and ended violently.

Odysseus, on the other hand, by virtue of his wits, will live to a ripe old age and is destined to die in peace.

THE PITFALLS OF TEMPTATION

The initial act that frustrated so many Achaeans' homecoming was the work of an Achaean himself: Ajax (the "Lesser" Ajax, a relatively unimportant figure not to be confused with the "Greater" Ajax, whom Odysseus meets in Hades) raped the Trojan priestess Cassandra in a temple while the Greeks were plundering the fallen city. That act of impulse, impiety, and stupidity brought the wrath of Athena upon the Achaean fleet and set in motion the chain of events that turned Odysseus's homecoming into a long nightmare. It is fit that *The Odyssey* is motivated by such an event, for many of the pitfalls that Odysseus and his men face are likewise obstacles that arise out of mortal weakness and the inability to control it. The submission to temptation or recklessness either angers the gods or distracts Odysseus and the members of his crew from their journey: they yield to hunger and slaughter the Sun's flocks, and they eat the fruit of the lotus and forget about their homes.

Even Odysseus's hunger for *kleos* is a kind of temptation. He submits to it when he reveals his name to Polyphemus, bringing Poseidon's wrath upon him and his men. In the case of the Sirens, the theme is revisited simply for its own interest. With their ears plugged, the crew members sail safely by the Sirens' island, while Odysseus, longing to hear the Sirens' sweet song, is saved from folly only by his foresighted command to his crew to keep him bound to the ship's mast. Homer is fascinated with depicting his protagonist tormented by temptation: in general, Odysseus and his men want very desperately to complete their *nostos,* or homecoming, but this desire is constantly at odds with the other pleasures that the world offers.

THEMES

MOTIFS

*Motifs are recurring structures, contrasts, and literary devices
that can help to develop and inform the text's major themes.*

STORYTELLING

Storytelling in *The Odyssey*, in addition to delivering the plot to the
audience, situates the epic in its proper cultural context. *The Odyssey*
seems very conscious of its predecessor, *The Iliad*: Odysseus's wanderings would never have taken place had he not left for Troy; and
The Odyssey would make little sense without *The Iliad* and the
knowledge that so many other Greek heroes had to make *nostoi*,
or homeward journeys, of their own. Homer constantly evokes the
history of *The Odyssey* through the stories that his characters tell.
Menelaus and Nestor both narrate to Telemachus their wanderings
from Troy. Even Helen adds some anecdotes about Odysseus's cunning during the Trojan War. Phemius, a court minstrel in Ithaca,
and Demodocus, a Phaeacian bard, sing of the exploits of the Greek
heroes at Troy. In the underworld, Agamemnon tells the story of his
murder, while Ajax's evasion prompts the story of his quarrel with
Odysseus. These stories, however, don't just provide colorful personal histories. Most call out to other stories in Greek mythology,
elevating *The Odyssey* by reminding its audience of the epic's rich,
mythic tradition.

DISGUISES

The gods of Greek literature often assume alternate forms to com-
mune with humans. In *The Odyssey*, Athena appears on earth disguised as everything from a little girl to Odysseus's friend Mentor
to Telemachus. Proteus, the Old Man of the Sea whom Menelaus
describes in Book 4, can assume any form, even water and fire, to
escape capture. Circe, on the other hand, uses her powers to change
others, turning an entire contingent of Odysseus's crew into pigs
with a tap of her wand.

From the first line of the epic, Homer explains that his story is
about a "man of twists and turns" (1.1). Quick, clever, and calculat-
ing, Odysseus is a natural master of disguise, and the plot of the epic
often turns on his deception. By withholding his true identity from
the Cyclops and using the alias "Nobody," for example, Odysseus
is able to save himself and his crew. But by revealing his name at
the end of this episode, Odysseus ends up being dogged by the god
Poseidon. His beggar disguise allows him to infiltrate his palace

and set up the final confrontation with the suitors. It also allows Homer to distinguish those who truly love Odysseus—characters like Eurycleia, Penelope, and even his dog, Argos, begin to recognize their beloved king even before he sheds his disguise.

SEDUCTRESSES

Women are very important figures in *The Odyssey,* and one of the most prominent roles they fulfill is that of seductress. Circe and Calypso are the most obvious examples of women whose love becomes an obstacle to Odysseus's return. Homer presents many other women whose irresistible allure threatens to lead men astray. The Sirens enchant Odysseus with their lovely song, and even Penelope, despite all of her contempt for the suitors, seems to be leading them on at times. She uses her feminine wiles to conceal her ruse of undoing, every night, her day's work on the burial shroud, and even gets the suitors to give her gifts, claiming that she will marry the one who gives her the nicest things. While these women do gain a certain amount of power through their sexual charms, they are ultimately all subject to divine whim, forced to wait and pine for love when it is absent.

SYMBOLS

Symbols are objects, characters, figures, and colors used to represent abstract ideas or concepts.

FOOD

Although throwing a feast for a guest is a common part of hospitality, hunger and the consumption of food often have negative associations in *The Odyssey.* They represent lack of discipline or submission to temptation, as when Odysseus tarries in the cave of the Cyclops, when his men slaughter the Sun's flocks, or when they eat the fruit of the lotus. The suitors, moreover, are constantly eating. Whenever Telemachus and Penelope complain about their uninvited guests, they mention how the suitors slaughter the palace's livestock. Odysseus kills the suitors just as they are starting their dinner, and Homer graphically describes them falling over tables and spilling their food. In almost all cases, the monsters of *The Odyssey* owe their monstrosity at least in part to their diets or the way that they eat. Scylla swallows six of Odysseus's men, one for each head. The Cyclops eats humans, but not sheep apparently, and is gluttonous nonetheless: when he gets drunk, he vomits up wine mixed with pieces of human flesh. The Laestrygonians seem like nice people—until their queen, who is described as "huge as a mountain crag," tries to eat Odysseus and his men (10.124). In these cases, excessive eating represents not just lack of self-control, but also the total absence of humanity and civility.

THE WEDDING BED

The wedding bed in Book 23 symbolizes the constancy of Penelope and Odysseus's marriage. Only a single maidservant has ever seen the bed, and it is where the happy couple spends its first night in each other's arms since Odysseus's departure for Troy twenty years earlier. The symbolism is heightened by the trick that Penelope uses to test Odysseus, which revolves around the immovability of their bed—a metaphor for the unshakable foundation of their love.

SYMBOLS

SUMMARY & ANALYSIS

BOOKS 1–2

SUMMARY: BOOK 1

Sing to me of the man, Muse, the man of twists and turns
driven time and again off course, once he had plundered
the hallowed heights of Troy.

(See QUOTATIONS, *p. 57)*

The narrator of *The Odyssey* invokes the Muse, asking for inspiration as he prepares to tell the story of Odysseus. The story begins ten years after the end of the Trojan War, the subject of *The Iliad*. All of the Greek heroes except Odysseus have returned home. Odysseus languishes on the remote island Ogygia with the goddess Calypso, who has fallen in love with him and refuses to let him leave. Meanwhile, a mob of suitors is devouring his estate in Ithaca and courting his wife, Penelope, in hopes of taking over his kingdom. His son, Telemachus, an infant when Odysseus left but now a young man, is helpless to stop them. He has resigned himself to the likelihood that his father is dead.

With the consent of Zeus, Athena travels to Ithaca to speak with Telemachus. Assuming the form of Odysseus's old friend Mentes, Athena predicts that Odysseus is still alive and that he will soon return to Ithaca. She advises Telemachus to call together the suitors and announce their banishment from his father's estate. She then tells him that he must make a journey to Pylos and Sparta to ask for any news of his father. After this conversation, Telemachus encounters Penelope in the suitors' quarters, upset over a song that the court bard is singing. Like Homer with *The Iliad,* the bard sings of the sufferings experienced by the Greeks on their return from Troy, and his song makes the bereaved Penelope more miserable than she already is. To Penelope's surprise, Telemachus rebukes her. He reminds her that Odysseus isn't the only Greek to not return from Troy and that, if she doesn't like the music in the men's quarters, she should retire to her own chamber and let him look after her interests among the suitors. He then gives the suitors notice that he will hold an assembly the next day at which they will be ordered to leave his father's estate. Antinous and Eurymachus, two particularly defiant suitors, rebuke Telemachus and ask the identity of the visitor with whom he has just been speaking. Although Telemachus suspects that his visitor was a goddess in disguise, he tells them only that the man was a friend of his father.

SUMMARY: BOOK 2

When the assembly meets the next day, Aegyptius, a wise Ithacan elder, speaks first. He praises Telemachus for stepping into his father's shoes, noting that this occasion marks the first time that the assembly has been called since Odysseus left. Telemachus then gives an impassioned speech in which he laments the loss of both his father and his father's home—his mother's suitors, the sons of Ithaca's elders, have taken it over. He rebukes them for consuming his father's oxen and sheep as they pursue their courtship day in and day out when any decent man would simply go to Penelope's father, Icarius, and ask him for her hand in marriage.

Antinous blames the impasse on Penelope, who, he says, seduces every suitor but will commit to none of them. He reminds the suitors of a ruse that she concocted to put off remarrying: Penelope maintained that she would choose a husband as soon as she finished weaving a burial shroud for her elderly father-in-law, Laertes. But each night, she carefully undid the knitting that she had completed during the day, so that the shroud would never be finished. If Penelope can make no decision, Antinous declares, then she should be sent back to Icarius so that he can choose a new husband for her. The dutiful Telemachus refuses to throw his mother out and calls upon the gods to punish the suitors. At that moment, a pair of eagles, locked in combat, appears overhead. The soothsayer Halitherses interprets their struggle as a portent of Odysseus's imminent return and warns the suitors that they will face a massacre if they don't leave. The suitors balk at such foolishness, and the meeting ends in deadlock.

As Telemachus is preparing for his trip to Pylos and Sparta, Athena visits him again, this time disguised as Mentor, another old friend of Odysseus. She encourages him and predicts that his journey will be fruitful. She then sets out to town and, assuming the disguise of Telemachus himself, collects a loyal crew to man his ship. Telemachus himself tells none of the household servants of his trip for fear that his departure will upset his mother. He tells only Eurycleia, his wise and aged nurse. She pleads with him not to take to the open sea as his father did, but he puts her fears to rest by saying that he knows that a god is at his side.

ANALYSIS: BOOKS 1–2

The Odyssey is an epic journey, but the word *journey* must be broadly understood. The epic focuses, of course, on Odysseus's *nostos* ("return home" or "homeward voyage"), a journey whose details a Greek audience would already know because of their rich oral mythic tradition. But Odysseus's return is not the only journey in *The Odyssey,* nor is it the one with which the story begins. After the opening passages, which explain Odysseus's situation, the focus shifts to the predicament of Odysseus's son, Telemachus. He finds himself coming of age in a household usurped by his mother's suitors, and it is he who, with the support of Athena and the other gods, must step into the role of household master that his father left vacant nearly twenty years earlier. Thus, in addition to a physical journey to Pylos and Sparta to learn more about his father's fate, Telemachus embarks upon a metaphorical journey into manhood to preserve his father's estate.

Like Homer's other epic, *The Iliad, The Odyssey* begins *in medias res,* or in the middle of things. Rather than open the story with the culmination of the Trojan War, Homer begins midway through Odysseus's wanderings. This presentation of events out of chronological sequence achieves several different goals: it immediately engages the interest of an audience already familiar with the details of Odysseus's journey; it provides narrative space for a long and evocative flashback later in the text (Books 9–12), in which Odysseus recounts his earlier travels; and it gives the story a satisfying unity when it ends where it began, at the house of Odysseus, in Book 24.

Most important, the *in medias res* opening infuses the foreground of the story with a sense of urgency. Were the narrative to begin with the happy victory over Troy and the beginning of Odysseus's trip back to Greece (a journey the Greeks would have expected to be brief at the time), the story would start at a high point and gradually descend as Odysseus's misfortunes increased. By commencing with a brief synopsis of Odysseus's whereabouts and then focusing on Telemachus's swift maturation, the narrator highlights the tension between Telemachus and the opportunistic suitors as it reaches a climax. Spurred on by the gods, Telemachus must confront the suitors to honor his father.

Telemachus has already begun his own psychological journey by the end of Book 1. Homer highlights his progress by showing how astounded the suitors are to be told so abruptly that they will have to leave the palace after the next day's assembly. Indeed, calling the assembly is itself a sign of Telemachus's awakening manhood, as Aegyptius notes at the beginning of Book 2. But even before his confrontation with the suitors, the confrontation between him and his mother reveals his new, surprisingly commanding outlook. When Penelope becomes upset at the bard's song, Telemachus chooses not to console her but rather to scold her. His unsympathetic treatment of her and his stiff reminder that Odysseus was not the only one who perished are stereotypically masculine responses to tragedy that suit him to the demands of running his father's household. He supplements these behavioral indications of manhood with the overt declaration, "I hold the reins of power in this house" (1.414).

Books 3–4

Summary: Book 3

At Pylos, Telemachus and Mentor (Athena in disguise) witness an impressive religious ceremony in which dozens of bulls are sacrificed to Poseidon, the god of the sea. Although Telemachus has little experience with public speaking, Mentor gives him the encouragement that he needs to approach Nestor, the city's king, and ask him about Odysseus. Nestor, however, has no information about the Greek hero. He recounts that after the fall of Troy a falling-out occurred between Agamemnon and Menelaus, the two Greek brothers who had led the expedition. Menelaus set sail for Greece immediately, while Agamemnon decided to wait a day and continue sacrificing on the shores of Troy. Nestor went with Menelaus, while Odysseus stayed with Agamemnon, and he has heard no news of Odysseus. He says that he can only pray that Athena will show Telemachus the kindness that she showed Odysseus. He adds that he has heard that suitors have taken over the prince's house in Ithaca and that he hopes that Telemachus will achieve the renown in defense of his father that Orestes, son of Agamemnon, won in defense of his father.

Telemachus then asks Nestor about Agamemnon's fate. Nestor explains that Agamemnon returned from Troy to find that Aegisthus, a base coward who remained behind while the Greeks fought in Troy, had seduced and married his wife, Clytemnestra. With her approval, Aegisthus murdered Agamemnon. He would have then taken over Agamemnon's kingdom had not Orestes, who was in exile in Athens, returned and killed Aegisthus and Clytemnestra. Nestor holds the courage of Orestes up as an example for Telemachus. He sends his own son Pisistratus along to accompany Telemachus to Sparta, and the two set out by land the next day. Athena, who reveals her divinity by shedding the form of Mentor and changing into an eagle before the entire court of Pylos, stays behind to protect Telemachus's ship and its crew.

SUMMARY: BOOK 4

In Sparta, the king and queen, Menelaus and Helen, are celebrating the separate marriages of their son and daughter. They happily greet Pisistratus and Telemachus, the latter of whom they soon recognize as the son of Odysseus because of the clear family resemblance. As they all feast, the king and queen recount with melancholy the many examples of Odysseus's cunning at Troy. Helen recalls how Odysseus dressed as a beggar to infiltrate the city's walls. Menelaus tells the famous story of the Trojan horse, Odysseus's masterful gambit that allowed the Greeks to sneak into Troy and slaughter the Trojans. The following day, Menelaus recounts his own return from Troy. He says that, stranded in Egypt, he was forced to capture Proteus, the divine Old Man of the Sea. Proteus told him the way back to Sparta and then informed him of the fates of Agamemnon and Ajax, another Greek hero, who survived Troy only to perish back in Greece. Proteus also told him news of Odysseus—that he was still alive but was imprisoned by Calypso on her island. Buoyed by this report, Telemachus and Pisistratus return to Pylos to set sail for Ithaca.

Meanwhile, the suitors at Odysseus's house learn of Telemachus's voyage and prepare to ambush him upon his return. The herald Medon overhears their plans and reports them to Penelope. She becomes distraught when she reflects that she may soon lose her son in addition to her husband, but Athena sends a phantom in the form of Penelope's sister, Iphthime, to reassure her. Iphthime tells her not to worry, for the goddess will protect Telemachus.

ANALYSIS: BOOKS 3–4

The setting broadens in Books 3 and 4 as Telemachus sets out on his own brief odyssey around southern Greece to learn of his father's fate. Fittingly, this expansion in setting prompts an expansion in the story itself, as each of Telemachus's hosts adds his own story to *The Odyssey*. Here, as throughout the poem, storytelling serves the important function of supplying both the reader and the characters with key details about Odysseus's travails. Additionally, Nestor's, Menelaus's, and Helen's recountings of various episodes related to the Trojan War tie *The Odyssey* to cultural legends with which Homer's audience would have been extremely familiar.

The stories that Telemachus now hears may have once coexisted with *The Iliad* and *The Odyssey* in the constellation of oral poetry that existed before either poem became a written work. A bard, much like the one depicted in Odysseus's palace, might sing of the exploits of Odysseus, Ajax, Agamemnon, or any of the other heroes whose stories circulated through early Greek culture in the form of oral poems. Like *The Iliad* and *Odyssey,* some of these poems may even have been written down at some point, though, if they were, they obviously didn't survive as long as Homer's two great epics. Still, Greek audiences would have been familiar with these stories, which were perhaps not just smaller stories embedded within *The Odyssey* but rather epics of their own. In any case, these stories were immediately and powerfully evocative, and by rehashing them Homer tethers his written rendition of *The Odyssey* to the tradition of epic narratives from which his work draws its inspiration.

Not surprisingly, the story that both Nestor and Menelaus recount—the cycle of murder in which Aegisthus killed Agamemnon and then Agamemnon's son, Orestes, killed Aegisthus—is clearly relevant to Telemachus. Just as Aegisthus took advantage of Agamemnon's absence to consort with his wife, so too have Penelope's suitors exploited Odysseus's presumed death to gorge themselves on his provisions and pursue his grieving wife. Telemachus's mission thus parallels that of Orestes: he must avenge his father by driving out the interlopers who have taken over his father's house. Nestor finds in the story of Agamemnon's fate a warning for Telemachus—that he shouldn't leave his home unguarded for too long, lest he return to find it stolen from him. The discovery, at the end of Book 4, that the suitors are plotting against Telemachus bears this lesson out.

Telemachus's meetings with the two kings also allow Homer to explore the idea of *xenia,* or hospitality. The social code of ancient Greece demanded that one show kindness to strangers in unfamiliar regions by welcoming them into one's home. This social expectation of hospitality was so culturally important that it was believed to be enforced by Zeus, the king of the gods. Here, both Nestor and Menelaus offer their guest a warm welcome even before they learn Telemachus's identity. Homer also emphasizes how impressed Menelaus is with his guest's discretion and tact ("Not even an older man could speak and do as well" [4.228]). This piety and respect for the social norms enforced by the gods contrasts sharply with the suitors' careless plundering of Telemachus's home in Ithaca in Books 1 and 2. While Telemachus strictly observes every divine law, the suitors carouse with wanton abandon, uninvited, in his home. While Telemachus impresses his hosts, the suitors plot to murder theirs. This exploration of the idea of hospitality thus provides a background against which the contrast between the suitors and Telemachus is sharpened, a contrast already emphasized by the frequent repetition of the story of Agamemnon.

BOOKS 5–6

SUMMARY: BOOK 5

> But if you only knew, down deep, what pains
> are fated to fill your cup before you reach that shore,
> you'd stay right here. . . .
> *(See* QUOTATIONS, *p. 58)*

All the gods except Poseidon gather again on Mount Olympus to discuss Odysseus's fate. Athena's speech in support of the hero prevails on Zeus to intervene. Hermes, messenger of the gods, is sent to Calypso's island to tell her that Odysseus must at last be allowed to leave so he can return home. In reply, Calypso delivers an impassioned indictment of the male gods and their double standards. She complains that they are allowed to take mortal lovers while the affairs of the female gods must always be frustrated. In the end, she submits to the supreme will of Zeus. By now, Odysseus alone remains of the contingent that he led at Troy; his crew and the other boats in his force were all destroyed during his journeys. Calypso helps him build a new boat and stocks it with provisions from her island. With sadness, she watches as the object of her love sails away.

After eighteen days at sea, Odysseus spots Scheria, the island of the Phaeacians, his next destination appointed by the gods. Just then, Poseidon, returning from a trip to the land of the Ethiopians, spots him and realizes what the other gods have done in his absence. Poseidon stirs up a storm, which nearly drags Odysseus under the sea, but the goddess Ino comes to his rescue. She gives him a veil that keeps him safe after his ship is wrecked. Athena too comes to his rescue as he is tossed back and forth, now out to the deep sea, now against the jagged rocks of the coast. Finally, a river up the coast of the island answers Odysseus's prayers and allows him to swim into its waters. He throws his protective veil back into the water as Ino had commanded him to do and walks inland to rest in the safe cover of a forest.

SUMMARY: BOOK 6

That night, Athena appears in a dream to the Phaeacian princess Nausicaa, disguised as her friend. She encourages the young princess to go to the river the next day to wash her clothes so that she will appear more fetching to the many men courting her. The next morning, Nausicaa goes to the river, and while she and her handmaidens are naked, playing ball as their clothes dry on the ground, Odysseus wakes in the forest and encounters them. Naked himself, he humbly yet winningly pleads for their assistance, never revealing his identity. Nausicaa leaves him alone to wash the dirt and brine from his body, and Athena makes him look especially handsome, so that when Nausicaa sees him again she begins to fall in love with him. Afraid of causing a scene if she walks into the city with a strange man at her side, Nausicaa gives Odysseus directions to the palace and advice on how to approach Arete, queen of the Phaeacians, when he meets her. With a prayer to Athena for hospitality from the Phaeacians, Odysseus sets out for the palace.

ANALYSIS: BOOKS 5–6

Our first encounter with Odysseus confirms what we have already learned about him from Menelaus's and Helen's accounts of his feats during the Trojan War and what Homer's audience would already have known: that Odysseus is very cunning and deliberative. The poet takes pains to show him weighing every decision: whether to try landing against the rocky coast of Scheria; whether to rest by the river or in the shelter of the woods; and whether to embrace Nausicaa's knees (the customary gesture of supplication) or address her from afar. The shrewd and measured approach that these instances demonstrate balances Odysseus's warrior mentality. Though aggressive and determined, he is far from rash. Instead, he is shrewd, cautious, and extremely self-confident. At one point, he even ignores the goddess Ino's advice to abandon ship, trusting in his seafaring abilities and declaring, "[I]t's what seems best to me" (5.397). In each case, he makes a decision and converts thought to action with speed and poise. In his encounter with Nausicaa, a telling example of his skill in interacting with people and charisma, his subdued approach comes off as "endearing, sly and suave" (6.162).

While these inner debates are characteristic of Odysseus, they are in some ways characteristic of *The Odyssey* as a whole. Unlike *The Iliad,* which explores the phenomena of human interaction—competition, aggression, warfare, and the glory that they can bring a man in the eyes of others—*The Odyssey* concerns itself much more with the unseen universe of the human heart, with feelings of loneliness, confusion, and despair. Not surprisingly, Homer introduces the hero Odysseus in a very unheroic way. We first find him sulking on a beach, yearning for home, alone except for the love-struck goddess who has imprisoned him there. Although not entirely foreign in *The Iliad,* this sort of pathetic scene still seems far removed from the grand, glorious battles of the first epic. Even without the linguistic and historical evidence, some commentators consider the stylistic divergence of scenes like this strong evidence of the separate authorship of these two poems.

Commentators are split in their interpretation of Calypso's extraordinary speech to the gods. Some see it as a realistic, unflinching account of the way things work in the patriarchal culture of ancient Greece: while men of the mortal world and Zeus and the other male gods can get away with promiscuous behavior, society expects females to be faithful at all times. Others understand Calypso's diatribe as a reaction to this reality. With this interpretation, we find ourselves naturally sympathetic to Calypso, who is making a passionate critique of social norms that are genuinely hypocritical. The question of interpretation becomes even trickier when we consider the relationship between Penelope and Odysseus. The poet seems to present Odysseus's affair with Calypso without rebuke while looking askance at Penelope's indulgence of the suitors, even though her faith in Odysseus never wavers. If we understand Calypso's speech as a criticism of these patriarchal norms, we can see how the text presents two contrary attitudes toward sexual behavior, and Calypso's speech seems to point out and condemn the unfair double standard that Homer seems to apply to Penelope.

BOOKS 7–8

SUMMARY: BOOK 7

On his way to the palace of Alcinous, the king of the Phaeacians, Odysseus is stopped by a young girl who is Athena in disguise. She offers to guide him to the king's house and shrouds him in a protective mist that keeps the Phaeacians, a kind but somewhat xenophobic people, from harassing him. She also advises him to direct his plea for help to Arete, the wise and strong queen who will know how to get him home. Once Athena has delivered Odysseus to the palace, she departs from Scheria to her beloved city of Athens.

Odysseus finds the palace residents holding a festival in honor of Poseidon. He is struck by the splendor of the palace and the king's opulence. As soon as he sees the queen, he throws himself at her feet, and the mist about him dissipates. At first, the king wonders if this wayward traveler might be a god, but without revealing his identity, Odysseus puts the king's suspicions to rest by declaring that he is indeed a mortal. He then explains his predicament, and the king and queen gladly promise to see him off the next day in a Phaeacian ship.

Later that evening, when the king and queen are alone with Odysseus, the wise Arete recognizes the clothes that he is wearing as ones that she herself had made for her daughter Nausicaa. Suspicious, she interrogates Odysseus further. While still withholding his name, Odysseus responds by recounting the story of his journey from Calypso's island and his encounter with Nausicaa that morning, which involved her giving him a set of clothes to wear. To absolve the princess for not accompanying him to the palace, Odysseus claims that it was his idea to come alone. Alcinous is so impressed with his visitor that he offers Odysseus his daughter's hand in marriage.

SUMMARY: BOOK 8

The next day, Alcinous calls an assembly of his Phaeacian counselors. Athena, back from Athens, ensures attendance by spreading word that the topic of discussion will be the godlike visitor who recently appeared on the island. At the assembly, Alcinous proposes providing a ship for his visitor so that the man can return to his homeland. The measure is approved, and Alcinous invites the counselors to his palace for a feast and celebration of games in honor of his guest. There, a blind bard named Demodocus sings of the quarrel between Odysseus and Achilles at Troy. Everyone listens with pleasure except Odysseus, who weeps at the painful memories that the story recalls. The king notices Odysseus's grief and ends the feast so that the games can begin.

The games include the standard lineup of boxing, wrestling, racing, and throwing of the discus. At one point, Odysseus is asked to participate. Still overcome by his many hardships, he declines. One of the young athletes, Broadsea, then insults him, which goads his pride to action. Odysseus easily wins the discus toss and then challenges the Phaeacian athletes to any other form of competition they choose. The discussion becomes heated, but Alcinous diffuses the situation by insisting that Odysseus join them in another feast, at which the Phaeacian youth entertain him and prove their preeminence in song and dance. Demodocus performs again, this time a light song about a tryst between Ares and Aphrodite. Afterward, Alcinous and each of the young Phaeacian men, including Broadsea, give Odysseus gifts to take with him on his journey home.

At dinner that night, Odysseus asks Demodocus to sing of the Trojan horse and the sack of Troy, but as he listens to the accomplished minstrel he again breaks down. King Alcinous again notices and stops the music. He asks Odysseus at last to tell him who he is, where he is from, and where he is going.

ANALYSIS: BOOKS 7–8

Odysseus's stay at Alcinous's palace provides the reader with some relief as it bridges the narrative of Odysseus's uncertain journey from Calypso's island and the woeful exploits that he recounts in Books 9 through 12. Ironically, for all of his poise, Odysseus cannot remain at peace even when he finds himself outside the direct influence of the wrath of various gods. His melancholy at the Phaeacian games prompts an insult from Broadsea, which in turn provokes an intense series of challenges between Odysseus and the Phaeacian youths. His tears at Demodocus's song attract Alcinous's attention and ultimately force him to reveal his identity and relate the history of his anguish-filled journey. Additionally, though he makes no mention of it again after Book 8, Homer has already hinted that Odysseus has aroused the affection of Princess Nausicaa—just a short while after escaping the demanding attentions of the divine Calypso.

The tension between passion and constancy is particularly strong in Books 7 and 8. Homer sustains it not only through subtle allusions to Nausicaa's blossoming love for Odysseus but also through Demodocus's rather unsubtle and greatly detailed song about the illicit affair between Ares and Aphrodite. Though its discussion of the planned trysts between the two lovers and the cleverly wrought trap used by Aphrodite's cheated husband, Hephaestus, to catch the adulterers in the act ends the song on a light note, the song clearly has relevance for the morose and dejected Odysseus. It invites us to recall his helpless transgression with Calypso and points to the future, when, like Hephaestus, Odysseus will take vengeance upon those who have tried to steal his bed.

The contrast between the Phaeacian youths' naïve glory-seeking and Odysseus's somberness despite having achieved considerable glory highlights how Odysseus's painful experiences have matured him. Inexperienced in life's hardships, the youths act rashly, as when Broadsea insults Odysseus, to attempt to demonstrate their man-hood. The exhortation of the youth Laodamas to Odysseus, "What greater glory attends a man . . . / than what he wins with his racing feet and striving hands? / . . . throw your cares to the wind!" illustrates the youths' simplistic preoccupation with physical prowess ("racing feet," "striving hands") (8.170–172). Odysseus, on the other hand, though clearly capable of besting the youths in athletic competition, exudes poise in the face of the youths' carefree bra-zenness, exerting himself only to defend his honor after Broadsea's insult. His retort that "[p]ains weigh on my spirit now, not your sports," displays his prioritization of the more grave concerns of family and loss over the trivial concern of glory for its own sake (8.178). Likewise, Nausicaa's immature attraction to Odysseus proves insignificant to him and cannot trump his desperate longing to return home.

Because he figures so prominently in the episode at Scheria and because the content of his first song so closely resembles that of *The Iliad,* commentators have often tried to equate the bard Demodocus with Homer. This interpretation, which seems to be the origin of the belief that Homer was blind, suggests that Homer inserts him-self into his own story. Though intriguing, we should remember that the performance of oral poetry played a much greater role in pre- or semiliterate cultures like the Greek world of *The Iliad* and *The Odyssey* than it does today or did even in the later, classical pe-riod of Greek history. While Demodocus's songs, such as that about Ares and Aphrodite, contribute much to our interpretation of *The Odyssey,* we should hesitate before concluding that they hold the key to decoding the identity of Homer. That Demodocus and his songs occupy a surprisingly large portion of Book 8 may owe simply to the culturally important role that oral poets played in Homeric life.

Book 9

Summary

Reluctantly, Odysseus tells the Phaeacians the sorry tale of his wanderings. From Troy, the winds sweep him and his men to Ismarus, city of the Cicones. The men plunder the land and, carried away by greed, stay until the reinforced ranks of the Cicones turn on them and attack. Odysseus and his crew finally escape, having lost six men per ship. A storm sent by Zeus sweeps them along for nine days before bringing them to the land of the Lotus-eaters, where the natives give some of Odysseus's men the intoxicating fruit of the lotus. As soon as they eat this fruit, they lose all thoughts of home and long for nothing more than to stay there eating more fruit. Only by dragging his men back to the ship and locking them up can Odysseus get them off the island.

Odysseus and his men then sail through the murky night to the land of the Cyclopes, a rough and uncivilized race of one-eyed giants. After making a meal of wild goats captured on an island offshore, they cross to the mainland. There they immediately come upon a cave full of sheep and crates of milk and cheese. The men advise Odysseus to snatch some of the food and hurry off, but, to his and his crew's detriment, he decides to linger. The cave's inhabitant soon returns—it is the Cyclops Polyphemus, the son of Poseidon. Polyphemus makes a show of hospitality at first, but he soon turns hostile. He devours two of Odysseus's men on the spot and imprisons Odysseus and the rest in his cave for future meals.

Odysseus wants to take his sword to Polyphemus right then, but he knows that only Polyphemus is strong enough to move the rock that he has placed across the door of his cave. Odysseus thus devises and executes a plan. The next day, while Polyphemus is outside pasturing his sheep, Odysseus finds a wooden staff in the cave and hardens it in the fire. When Polyphemus returns, Odysseus gets him drunk on wine that he brought along from the ship. Feeling jovial, Polyphemus asks Odysseus his name. Odysseus replies that his name is "Nobody" (9.410). As soon as Polyphemus collapses with intoxication, Odysseus and a select group of his men drive the red-hot staff into his eye. Polyphemus wakes with a shriek, and his neighbors come to see what is wrong, but they leave as soon as he calls out, "Nobody's killing me" (9.455). When morning comes, Odysseus and his men escape from the cave, unseen by the blind Polyphemus, by clinging to the bellies of the monster's sheep as they go out to graze. Safe on board their ships and with Polyphemus's flock on board as well, Odysseus calls to land and reveals his true identity. With his former prisoners now out of reach, the blind giant lifts up a prayer to his father, Poseidon, calling for vengeance on Odysseus.

ANALYSIS

Books 9 through 12 are told as flashbacks, as Odysseus sits in the palace of the Phaeacians telling the story of his wanderings. These books thus give background not only to Odysseus's audience but to Homer's as well. Providing some of the richest and most celebrated examples of Odyssean cunning, they speak as much to the resourcefulness of the poet, who uses Odysseus's voice to render a more complete picture of his hero's wanderings, as to that of the hero himself. The foreboding that Odysseus feels as he heads toward the cave, which seems to prompt him to take the wine along, foreshadows his upcoming encounter with Polyphemus and the need for trickery to prevail. Once Homer establishes the conflict between Odysseus and Polyphemus, he unveils Odysseus's escape plan slowly and subtly: the significance of Odysseus's blinding of Polyphemus becomes clear when Polyphemus lets his sheep out to graze the next morning; similarly, Odysseus's curious lie about his name seems nonsense at first but adds a clever and humorous twist to the necessity of keeping the other Cyclopes from rescuing Polyphemus.

Odysseus's eventual revelation of his identity to Polyphemus ultimately proves foolish, and, because it embodies a lack of foresight, stands in stark contrast to the cunning prudence that Odysseus displays in his plan to escape from the cave. Though his anger at Polyphemus for devouring his shipmates is certainly understandable, and though Polyphemus's blind rock-throwing fury eggs him on, Odysseus's taunts are unnecessary. By telling Polyphemus his name, Odysseus pits his mortal indignation against Poseidon's divine vengeance. This act of hubris, or excessive pride, ensures almost automatically that Odysseus will suffer grave consequences. Indeed, his eventual punishment costs him dearly: Poseidon's anger wipes away the very thing that he gains by cleverly obscuring his name—the safety of his men.

The form that Odysseus's revelation of his identity takes is interesting, as it represents the cultural values of ancient Greece.

Odysseus doesn't simply utter his name; rather, he attaches to it an epithet, or short, descriptive title ("raider of cities"), his immediate paternal ancestry ("Laertes's son"), and a reference to his homeland ("who makes his home in Ithaca") (9.561–562). This manner of introduction was very formalized and formulaic in Homeric Greece and should seem familiar to readers of *The Iliad*. Odysseus is here going through the motions of confirming his kleos (the glory or renown that one earns in the eyes of others by performing great deeds). He wants to make sure that people know that he was the one who blinded Polyphemus, explicitly instructing Polyphemus to make others aware of his act. Like the heroes of *The Iliad*, Odysseus believes that the height of glory is achieved by spreading his name abroad through great deeds.

For all of his stupidity and brutishness, Polyphemus strikes some commentators as vaguely sympathetic at the end of Book 9. They point to the pitiful prayer that he offers to his father, Poseidon, and his warm treatment of his beloved sheep, who are soon to be devoured by Odysseus and his men. He caresses each wooly back as it passes out of his cave, and it is difficult not to pity him when he gives special attention to his faithful lead ram. Homer notes that, "[s]troking him gently, powerful Polyphemus murmured, / 'Dear old ram, why last of the flock to quit the cave?'" (9.497–498). The juxtaposition of "gently" and "powerful" and the poetically stated question illustrate that, despite his monstrousness, Polyphemus is somewhat tenderhearted. Additionally, in pondering why the ram is the last to leave the cave, Polyphemus attributes a human capacity for sympathy to him ("Sick at heart for your master's eye" [9.505]). His tenderness is all the more endearing for his ignorance—he is wholly unaware of Odysseus's cunning. Though Homeric culture praised Odysseus for his characteristic cunning, others have criticized him for this quality, perceiving his tactics as conniving, underhanded, dishonest, and even cowardly. Dante, for example, in the *Inferno*, relegates Odysseus to the Eighth Pouch of the Eighth Circle of Hell—the realm reserved for those guilty of Spiritual Theft—because of his treachery in the Trojan horse episode that enabled him to slaughter the unwitting Trojans.

BOOKS 10–11

SUMMARY: BOOK 10

The Achaeans sail from the land of the Cyclopes to the home of Aeolus, ruler of the winds. Aeolus presents Odysseus with a bag containing all of the winds, and he stirs up a westerly wind to guide Odysseus and his crew home. Within ten days, they are in sight of Ithaca, but Odysseus's shipmates, who think that Aeolus has secretly given Odysseus a fortune in gold and silver, tear the bag open. The winds escape and stir up a storm that brings Odysseus and his men back to Aeolia. This time, however, Aeolus refuses to help them, certain that the gods hate Odysseus and wish to do him harm.

Lacking wind, the Achaeans row to the land of the Laestrygonians, a race of powerful giants whose king, Antiphates, and unnamed queen turn Odysseus's scouts into dinner. Odysseus and his remaining men flee toward their ships, but the Laestrygonians pelt the ships with boulders and sink them as they sit in the harbor. Only Odysseus's ship escapes.

From there, Odysseus and his men travel to Aeaea, home of the beautiful witch-goddess Circe. Circe drugs a band of Odysseus's men and turns them into pigs. When Odysseus goes to rescue them, Hermes approaches him in the form of a young man. He tells Odysseus to eat an herb called moly to protect himself from Circe's drug and then lunge at her when she tries to strike him with her sword. Odysseus follows Hermes' instructions, overpowering Circe and forcing her to change his men back to their human forms. Odysseus soon becomes Circe's lover, and he and his men live with her in luxury for a year. When his men finally persuade him to continue the voyage homeward, Odysseus asks Circe for the way back to Ithaca. She replies he must sail to Hades, the realm of the dead, to speak with the spirit of Tiresias, a blind prophet who will tell him how to get home.

The next morning, Odysseus rouses his men for the imminent departure. He discovers, however, that the youngest man in his crew, Elpenor, had gotten drunk the previous night, slept on the roof, and, when he heard the men shouting and marching in the morning, fell from the roof and broke his neck. Odysseus explains to his men the course that they must take, which they are displeased to learn is rather meandering.

SUMMARY: BOOK 11

By god, I'd rather slave on earth for another man . . .
than rule down here over all the breathless dead.

(See QUOTATIONS, *p. 59*)

Odysseus travels to the River of Ocean in the land of the Cimmerians. There he pours libations and performs sacrifices as Circe earlier instructs him to do to attract the souls of the dead. The first to appear is that of Elpenor, the crewman who broke his neck falling from Circe's roof. He begs Odysseus to return to Circe's island and give his body a proper burial. Odysseus then speaks with the Theban prophet Tiresias, who reveals that Poseidon is punishing the Achaeans for blinding his son Polyphemus. He foretells Odysseus's fate—that he will return home, reclaim his wife and palace from the wretched suitors, and then make another trip to a distant land to appease Poseidon. He warns Odysseus not to touch the flocks of the Sun when he reaches the land of Thrinacia; otherwise, he won't return home without suffering much more hardship and losing all of his crew. When Tiresias departs, Odysseus calls other spirits toward him. He speaks with his mother, Anticleia, who updates him on the affairs of Ithaca and relates how she died of grief waiting for his return. He then meets the spirits of various famous men and heroes and hears the stories of their lives and deaths.

Odysseus now cuts short the tale and asks his Phaeacian hosts to allow him to sleep, but the king and queen urge him to continue, asking if he met any of the Greeks who fell at Troy in Hades. He relates his encounters there: he meets Agamemnon, who tells him of his murder at the hands of his wife, Clytemnestra. Next he meets Achilles, who asks about his son, Neoptolemus. Odysseus then tries to speak with Ajax, an Achaean who killed himself after he lost a contest with Odysseus over the arms of Achilles, but Ajax refuses to speak and slips away. He sees Heracles, King Minos, the hunter Orion, and others. He witnesses the punishment of Sisyphus, struggling eternally to push a boulder over a hill only to have it roll back down whenever it reaches the top. He then sees Tantalus, agonized by hunger and thirst. Tantalus sits in a pool of water overhung by bunches of grapes, but whenever he reaches for the grapes, they rise out of grasp, and whenever he bends down to drink, the water sinks out of reach. Odysseus soon finds himself mobbed by souls wishing to ask about their relatives in the world above. He becomes frightened, runs back to his ship, and immediately sails away.

ANALYSIS: BOOKS 10–11

The mortal tendency to succumb to temptation manifests itself throughout Book 10. Just as Odysseus taunts the blinded Polyphemus in book 9 by boasting about his defeat of the Cyclops, the members of his crew prove unable to resist looking into Aeolus's bag, and their greed ends up complicating their *nostos,* or homeward voyage. As important and illustrative of weak-mindedness, however, is that Odysseus lets a year waste away in the arms of the goddess Circe. While his crew certainly seems not to mind the respite, Odysseus particularly enjoys it, even though his wife is waiting for him. The drunk Elpenor's death as the men are about to depart from home constitutes another instance of overindulgence in personal appetite.

Only when his crew "prod[s]" him and calls his delays "madness" is Odysseus persuaded to leave Circe's realm (10.519–520). The crew members' lukewarm feelings for the place are understandable—after all, they have to suffer the humiliation of being transformed, initially, into pigs and receive no recompense comparable to the love of a goddess. Indeed, in Book 10, for the first time we hear the crew criticize its leader. Refusing repeatedly to return to Circe's halls after the other scouts are transformed into pigs, the crew member Eurylochus issues an especially stinging reproach of Odysseus for foolishly leading his crew to its destruction. He presents the death of their comrades at the hands of Polyphemus as evidence of Odysseus's imprudence: "thanks to [Odysseus's] rashness they died too!" (10.482). Though Odysseus checks his anger and restores calm, the unrest illustrates the holes in his authority.

With the appearance of the various heroes and lesser divinities, Book 11 gives the modern reader an extraordinary anthology of mythological lives. Homer's audience would already have been familiar with the stories of such figures as Heracles, Minos, Achilles, Agamemnon, Sisyphus, and Tantalus, and people turned to them for authoritative versions of the Greek myths even in the later ancient period. For the modern reader, they provide invaluable insight into early Greek mythology. Again, by juxtaposing Odysseus's wanderings to the woes of these legendary figures, Homer both broadens the scope of his poem and further entrenches his hero in his culture's mythology. In even being allowed to enter Hades, Odysseus attains a privileged, transcendent status.

Odysseus's conversation with Achilles reveals a nuanced view of warfare and *kleos,* or glory, which is harder to find in *The Iliad.* Achilles' declaration, "I'd rather slave on earth for another man / . . . / than rule down here over all the breathless dead," alludes to his dilemma, depicted in *The Iliad,* of choosing between earning glory on the battlefield but dying young and living out a long, uneventful life (11.556–558). Whereas *The Iliad,* which celebrates the glory of warfare, wholeheartedly endorses Achilles' choice of glory over long life, Achilles' lament in Book 11 of *The Odyssey* issues a strong caveat to this ethic of *kleos.* This change in Achilles' sentiment from one poem to the next is understandable, given that, as we have seen with Odysseus, *The Odyssey* tends to focus on characters' inner lives. Yet Achilles doesn't wholly shun the idea of *kleos.* Though he turns away somewhat from his warrior ethos, he still rejoices to hear that his son has become a great warrior. *Kleos* has thus evolved from an accepted cultural value into a more complex and somewhat problematic principle.

Positioned near the very heart of the epic, the underworld segment ties together the poem's various settings. Anticleia recalls those pining away for Odysseus in Ithaca. Agamemnon and Achilles shift our thoughts back to Troy. Elpenor ties in the near past on Circe's island and the present responsibilities that Odysseus has to his crew. Finally, the interruption in Odysseus's account reminds us of where he is now—in the palace of the Phaeacians. The interruption seems to have no other function, and it doesn't make much sense within the context of the plot. It is hard to believe, for instance, that Odysseus would want to go to sleep before describing the most important conversations he had in Hades, and, in fact, he doesn't go to sleep—the history of his wanderings goes on for another book and a half. The interruption is transparently used to break the long first-person narrative into smaller, more manageable chunks.

Books 12–14

Summary: Book 12

Odysseus returns to Aeaea, where he buries Elpenor and spends one last night with Circe. She describes the obstacles that he will face on his voyage home and tells him how to negotiate them. As he sets sail, Odysseus passes Circe's counsel on to his men. They approach the island of the lovely Sirens, and Odysseus, as instructed by Circe, plugs his men's ears with beeswax and has them bind him to the mast of the ship. He alone hears their song flowing forth from the island, promising to reveal the future. The Sirens' song is so seductive that Odysseus begs to be released from his fetters, but his faithful men only bind him tighter.

Once they have passed the Sirens' island, Odysseus and his men must navigate the straits between Scylla and Charybdis. Scylla is a six-headed monster who, when ships pass, swallows one sailor for each head. Charybdis is an enormous whirlpool that threatens to swallow the entire ship. As instructed by Circe, Odysseus holds his course tight against the cliffs of Scylla's lair. As he and his men stare at Charybdis on the other side of the strait, the heads of Scylla swoop down and gobble up six of the sailors.

Odysseus next comes to Thrinacia, the island of the Sun. He wants to avoid it entirely, but the outspoken Eurylochus persuades him to let his beleaguered crew rest there. A storm keeps them beached for a month, and at first the crew is content to survive on its provisions in the ship. When these run out, however, Eurylochus persuades the other crew members to disobey Odysseus and slaughter the cattle of the Sun. They do so one afternoon as Odysseus sleeps; when the Sun finds out, he asks Zeus to punish Odysseus and his men. Shortly after the Achaeans set sail from Thrinacia, Zeus kicks up another storm, which destroys the ship and sends the entire crew to its death beneath the waves. As had been predicted, only Odysseus survives, and he just barely. The storm sweeps him all the way back to Charybdis, which he narrowly escapes for the second time. Afloat on the broken timbers of his ship, he eventually reaches Ogygia, Calypso's island. Odysseus here breaks from his story, stating to the Phaeacians that he sees no reason to repeat to them his account of his experience on Ogygia.

SUMMARY: BOOK 13

The account of his wanderings now finished, Odysseus looks forward to leaving Scheria. The next day, Alcinous loads his gifts on board the ship that will carry Odysseus to Ithaca. Odysseus sets sail as soon as the sun goes down. He sleeps the whole night, while the Phaeacian crew commands the ship. He remains asleep even when the ship lands the next morning. The crew gently carries him and his gifts to shore and then sails for home.

When Poseidon spots Odysseus in Ithaca, he becomes enraged at the Phaeacians for assisting his nemesis. He complains to Zeus, who allows him to punish the Phaeacians. Just as their ship is pulling into harbor at Scheria, the prophecy mentioned at the end of Book 8 is fulfilled: the ship suddenly turns to stone and sinks to the bottom of the sea. The onlookers ashore immediately recognize the consummation of the prophecy and resolve to abandon their custom of helping wayward travelers.

Back in Ithaca, Odysseus wakes to find a country that he doesn't recognize, for Athena has shrouded it in mist to conceal its true form while she plans his next move. At first, he curses the Phaeacians, whom he thinks have duped him and left him in some unknown land. But Athena, disguised as a shepherd, meets him and tells him that he is indeed in Ithaca. With characteristic cunning, Odysseus acts to conceal his identity from her until she reveals hers. Delighted by Odysseus's tricks, Athena announces that it is time for Odysseus to use his wits to punish the suitors. She tells him to hide out in the hut of his swineherd, Eumaeus. She informs him that Telemachus has gone in search of news of him and gives him the appearance of an old vagabond so that no one will recognize him.

SUMMARY: BOOK 14

Odysseus finds Eumaeus outside his hut. Although Eumaeus doesn't recognize the withered traveler as his master, he invites him inside. There Odysseus has a hearty meal of pork and listens as Eumaeus heaps praise upon the memory of his former master, whom he fears is lost for good, and scorn upon the behavior of his new masters, the vile suitors. Odysseus predicts that Eumaeus will see his master again quite soon, but Eumaeus will hear none of it—he has encountered too many vagabonds looking for a handout from Penelope in return for fabricated news of Odysseus. Still, Eumaeus takes a liking to his guest. He puts him up for the night and even lets him borrow a cloak to keep out the cold. When Eumaeus asks Odysseus about his origins, Odysseus lies that he is from Crete. He fought with Odysseus at Troy and made it home safely, he claims, but a trip that he made later to Egypt went awry, and he was reduced to poverty. It was during this trip, he says, that he heard that Odysseus was still alive.

ANALYSIS: BOOKS 12–13

Like much of *The Odyssey,* Book 12 generates excitement through the tension between goals and obstacles. Some of these obstacles are simply unpleasant: Odysseus would rather avoid Scylla and Charybdis altogether, but he cannot—they stand in his way, leaving him no choice but to navigate a path through them. But many of these obstacles are temptations. Unlike Scylla and Charybdis, the island of Thrinacia poses no immediate threat to Odysseus or his men. While the cautious Odysseus advocates resisting the urge even to land on Thrinacia, the crew's instincts and desires drive them to slaughter the Sun's flocks even after promising Odysseus that they wouldn't do so. Even Odysseus's experience with the Sirens is a study in temptation, a temptation that Odysseus keeps in check through foresight. The picture that Homer paints of Odysseus strapped to the mast, begging to be released, is symbolic of many of his and his crew's experiences on the seas. Immediate, visceral desires distract him from his *nostos,* or homeward journey, but a deeper longing and a more intellectual understanding of his mission's importance keep him tied to his course.

Some scholars believe that the straits between Scylla and Charybdis represent the Straits of Messina, which lie between Sicily and mainland Italy, as these straits are a prominent geographical feature and indeed treacherous to navigate. But Homeric geography is notoriously problematic. Separate efforts to map Odysseus's wanderings often place the same destination in different hemispheres of the globe. Things become convoluted even on mainland Greece, as Homer often misjudges distances and even invents geographical features. Bearing these issues in mind, it is entirely possible that Homer neither knew nor cared about the location of the straits that inspired his Scylla and Charybdis episode—or that they were simply the creations of his and his predecessors' imaginations.

Book 13 picks up where Book 4 left off: the setting quickly shifts back to Ithaca and the suitors again dominate the background of the story. No sooner does Odysseus forget the Phaeacians than he and Athena are conspiring to destroy the mob that has taken over his house, refocusing the poem from stories of misadventure in the past to the central tension in the present. Athena's mention of Telemachus's wanderings also gives the narrative a sense of continuity with the poem's earlier books.

Athena's description of this trip shows once again how significantly *kleos,* or glory, figures in Homer's world. For if Athena knew of Odysseus's plight and imminent return, it seems illogical, at first, that she would send Telemachus on such a risky trip. While Telemachus's journey proves instrumental in the maturation already under way in Books 1 and 2, Athena states that the purpose of his going to Pylos and Sparta was for him to "make his name by sailing there" (13.482). She is more interested in how performing great deeds in faraway lands will elevate his reputation than in his inner, more personal growth. Throughout *The Odyssey*, Athena shows a steadfast devotion to Odysseus and the traits that he embodies; in risking his life to find his father, Telemachus stands to gain a measure of that same renown for which Odysseus and other Greek heroes risked their lives at Troy.

The destruction of the Phaeacian vessel raises an exception to *xenia,* the Homeric code of hospitality. As Bernard Knox argues in the introduction to Robert Fagles's translation of *The Odyssey,* the obligation of assisting and entertaining travelers and wayfarers is the closest *The Odyssey* comes to asserting an absolute moral principle. Zeus, king of the gods, is depicted as the enforcer of this code of hospitality. Yet he sanctions Poseidon's punishment of the Phaeacians, who anger Poseidon precisely by following, even exceeding, this code in helping Odysseus to return home. This code, it seems, applies only as long as the egos of gods are not bruised. Zeus's submission to Poseidon's desire for revenge supports Fagles's claim that the most powerful gods never allow human concerns—the interests of the people whom they favor—to precipitate conflict among themselves. The gods elect to use alliance, deceit, and diplomatic negotiation to play out their power struggles rather than allow them to degenerate into open conflict. For Zeus, preserving stable relations with his brother is more important than returning favors to one of his most suppliant peoples.

BOOKS 15–16

SUMMARY: BOOK 15

Athena travels to Sparta, where she finds Telemachus and Pisistratus, Nestor's son, asleep in Menelaus's palace. She appears to Telemachus in a dream and tells him that he must hurry home to Ithaca before the suitors succeed in winning his mother's hand. She also warns him of the ambush that they have set and explains how to avoid it. Finally, she instructs him to head first for the home of the swineherd Eumaeus, who will convey the news of his safe return to Penelope.

The next day, Telemachus announces his departure and accepts gifts from Menelaus and Helen. As Telemachus pulls away from the palace in his chariot, an eagle carrying a goose stolen from a pen swoops down beside him. Helen interprets the incident as an omen that Odysseus is about to swoop down on his home and exact revenge on the suitors.

Once at Pylos, Telemachus has Pisistratus drop him off at his ship, insisting that he has no time to spare to visit Nestor again. The ship is about to set off when Theoclymenus, a famous prophet's descendant who is fleeing prosecution for a crime of manslaughter that he committed in Argos, approaches Telemachus and asks to come aboard. Telemachus welcomes him and offers him hospitality when they get to Ithaca.

In the hut of Eumaeus, Odysseus tests the limit of his hospitality by offering to leave in the morning, a false gesture that he hopes will prompt Eumaeus to offer to let him stay longer. He urges the old man not to go out of his way and says that he will earn his keep working for the suitors, but Eumaeus will have none of it. To get mixed up with those suitors, he warns, would be suicide. Odysseus and the swineherd then swap stories. Eumaeus explains how he first came to Ithaca: the son of a king, he was stolen from his house by Phoenician pirates with the help of a maid that his father employed. The pirates took him all over the seas until Laertes, Odysseus's father, bought him in Ithaca. There, Laertes' wife brought him up alongside her own daughter, the youngest born.

The next morning, Telemachus reaches the shores of Ithaca. He disembarks while the crew heads to the city by ship. He entrusts Theoclymenus to a loyal crewman, Piraeus. As they part, they see a hawk fly by carrying a dove in its talons, which Theoclymenus interprets as a favorable sign of the strength of Odysseus's house and line.

SUMMARY: BOOK 16

When Telemachus reaches Eumaeus's hut, he finds the swineherd talking with a stranger (Odysseus in disguise). Eumaeus recounts Odysseus's story and suggests that the stranger stay with Telemachus at the palace. But Telemachus is afraid of what the suitors might do to them. Eumaeus thus goes to the palace alone to tell Penelope that her son has returned.

When father and son are alone in the hut, Athena appears to Odysseus and calls him outside. When Odysseus reenters the hut, his old-man disguise is gone, and he stands in the pristine glory of his heroic person. At first, Telemachus cannot believe his eyes, but then the two embrace and weep. Odysseus recounts his trip with the Phaeacians and then begins plotting the overthrow of the suitors. He formulates a plan to launch a surprise attack from within the palace: Odysseus will enter disguised as a beggar and Telemachus will hide the palace's surplus arms where the suitors cannot easily reach them. The two of them will then seize the arms and slaughter the suitors.

Before Eumaeus can give Penelope news of Telemachus's return, the messenger from the ship arrives and informs the entire palace that Telemachus has returned. The suitors, dejected that their plot has failed, huddle outside to plan their next move. Antinous recommends putting Telemachus to death before he can call an assembly at which the suitors' dirty schemes can be aired, but Amphinomus, one of the more thoughtful and well-behaved suitors, persuades the others to wait for a sign from the gods before doing anything so rash. Penelope later finds Antinous in the palace and denounces him for the plot against her son, the details of which Medon had overheard and revealed to her in Book 4. Eurymachus succeeds in calming Penelope down with his lies and false concern for the safety of Telemachus.

ANALYSIS: BOOKS 15–16

In Books 15 and 16, the plot becomes much more complicated, as Homer plants details and characters crucial for bringing the story to its climax. For the first time in the poem, the paths of Odysseus and Telemachus converge. Athena must have them meet in the privacy of Eumaeus's hut—a meeting in the palace might be suspicious, since princes and beggars have no reason to interact with each other—so that Odysseus can reveal his identity to his son without endangering his plans to exact vengeance upon the suitors. From a literary standpoint, the tender irony of a king and prince reuniting in the lowly hut of a swineherd reaffirms these men's human qualities. They are not simply the emotionless figures of established and budding hero, respectively, but rather emotional individuals with interior lives.

Up until the suitors' discovery of Telemachus's return, Homer has generally refrained from individualizing the suitors; they work much better as an undifferentiated mass of degenerate, one-dimensional characters with whom we have no desire to sympathize. But in the suitors' ensuing debate, two sides emerge: one, whose spokesman is Antinous, is predictably thuggish; the other, however, advocates a more thoughtful and moderate position. To represent this latter side, Homer introduces the suitor Amphinomus, who is thoughtful, pious, and eager to see what the gods think before doing anything rash; additionally, he is one of Penelope's favorites. These positive attributes complicate the justness of Odysseus's revenge, as the suitors are no longer exclusively faceless villains; Odysseus's revenge will come at the expense not only of the truly malevolent suitors but also of the few who are not wholly bad individuals.

Helen's and Theoclymenus's interpretations of the separate bird omens rely on the perception of Odysseus as an aggressive, predatory creature: in each incident, a more powerful, regal bird (eagle, hawk) asserts its superiority over a more common, vulnerable one (goose, dove). Just as these rapacious birds swoop down upon their unsuspecting prey, so too, the interpretations imply, will Odysseus pounce upon the suitors without warning. Ancient Greek culture revered omens as indications of unalterable divine will, and the prophet Theoclymenus, whom Telemachus finds, begins to play an important role. Over the next few books, the number of omens in need of interpretation rises dramatically, as Homer increasingly depicts the suitors as condemned men and ever more explicitly foreshadows their impending doom.

Homer continues exploring how the extension of, and reaction to, *xenia,* or hospitality, reflects various characters' concerns. Nestor's insistence that Telemachus stay and feast with him in Pylos before returning to Ithaca confirms that he is a commendable, godsfearing man. Telemachus's eagerness to avoid this social commitment may seem a breach of social propriety, but, in desiring not to delay his return further, he resembles his shrewd father. His evasion is justified by his prioritizing of practical considerations—the need to return home quickly—over decorum and other formal considerations. Besides, Telemachus's warm reception of Theoclymenus, in addition to the genuine urgency of the moment, takes some of the edge off of his apparent inconsiderateness.

Books 17–18

Summary: Book 17

Telemachus leaves Odysseus at Eumaeus's hut and heads to his palace, where he receives a tearful welcome from Penelope and the nurse Eurycleia. In the palace hall he meets Theoclymenus and Piraeus. He tells Piraeus not to bring his gifts from Menelaus to the palace; he fears that the suitors will steal them if they kill him. When he sits down to eat with Penelope, Telemachus tells her what little news he received of Odysseus in Pylos and Sparta, but he doesn't reveal that he has seen Odysseus with his own eyes in Eumaeus's hut. Theoclymenus then speaks up and swears that Odysseus is in Ithaca at this very moment.

Meanwhile, Eumaeus and Odysseus set out toward town in Telemachus's footsteps. On the way they meet Melanthius, a base subordinate of the suitors, who heaps scorn on Eumaeus and kicks his beggar companion. Odysseus receives a similar welcome at the palace. The suitors give him food with great reluctance, and Antinous goes out of his way to insult him. When Odysseus answers insult with insult, Antinous gives him a blow with a stool that disgusts even the other suitors. Report of this cruelty reaches Penelope, who asks to have the beggar brought to her so that she can question him about Odysseus. Odysseus, however, doesn't want the suitors to see him heading toward the queen's room. Eumaeus announces that he must return to his hut and hogs, leaving Odysseus alone with Telemachus and the suitors.

Summary: Book 18

> Of all that breathes and crawls across the earth,
> Our mother earth breeds nothing feebler than a man.
> *(See* QUOTATIONS, *p. 60)*

Another beggar, Arnaeus (nicknamed Irus), saunters into the palace. For a beggar, he is rather brash: he insults Odysseus and challenges him to a boxing match. He thinks that he will make quick work of the old man, but Athena gives Odysseus extra strength and stature. Irus soon regrets challenging the old man and tries to escape, but by now the suitors have taken notice and are egging on the fight for the sake of their own entertainment. It ends quickly as Odysseus floors Irus and stops just short of killing him.

The suitors congratulate Odysseus. One in particular, the moderate Amphinomus, toasts him and gives him food. Odysseus, fully aware of the bloodshed to come and overcome by pity for Amphinomus, pulls the man aside. He predicts to Amphinomus that Odysseus will soon be home and gives him a thinly veiled warning to abandon the palace and return to his own land. But Amphinomus doesn't depart, despite being "fraught with grave forebodings," for Athena has bound him to death at the hands of Telemachus (18.176).

Athena now puts it into Penelope's head to make an appearance before her suitors. The goddess gives her extra stature and beauty to inflame their hearts. When Penelope speaks to the suitors, she leads them on by telling them that Odysseus had instructed her to take a new husband if he should fail to return before Telemachus began growing facial hair. She then tricks them, to the silent delight of Odysseus, into bringing her gifts by claiming that any suitor worth his salt would try to win her hand by giving things to her instead of taking what's rightfully hers. The suitors shower her with presents, and, as they celebrate, Odysseus instructs the maidservants to go to Penelope. The maidservant Melantho, Melanthius's sister, insults him as an inferior being and a drunk; Odysseus then scares them off with threats. Hoping to make Odysseus even more angry at the suitors, Athena now inspires Eurymachus to insult him. When Odysseus responds with insults of his own, Eurymachus throws a stool at him but misses, hitting a servant instead. Just as a riot is about to break out, Telemachus steps in and diffuses the situation, to the consternation of the suitors.

ANALYSIS: BOOKS 17–18

Homer uses minor characters of low rank to great effect in Books 17 and 18. Like many Homeric characters, neither the swineherd Melanthius nor the maidservant Melantho is very developed. They are little more than male and female versions of the same malevolent person: each ostensibly works for Odysseus but has become a partisan of the suitors. Despite their simplicity, they function as foils—characters whose traits or attitudes contrast with and thereby accentuate those of other characters. Melanthius's disrespectful treatment of Odysseus stands in stark contrast to Eumaeus's unflinching loyalty to his master. Similarly, in contrast to the devoted Eurycleia, Melantho proves the embodiment of ingratitude toward Penelope: though Penelope raised her like her own child, Melantho shows no concern for Penelope's grief. Additionally, Irus's mingled bravado and cowardice provide a good foil for Odysseus's prudence and courage. Homer also uses Irus to foreshadow the ultimate downfall of the suitors: disguised as a beggar, Odysseus cuts down an impudent beggar, leaving little doubt as to what he will do to the impudent nobles when he reassumes his noble form. The foreshadowing is not lost on the suitor Amphinomus, who walks away stony with dread.

Amphinomus provides another case study in the absolute power of the gods. Even though Amphinomus shows some kindness toward the seeming beggar, Odysseus pities him, and Homer singles him out as the one moderate and thoughtful man among all of the suitors, nothing can save him from the punishment that Athena has planned for him. In fact, Athena doesn't even take his benevolence into consideration. Homer explains that "[e]ven then Athena had bound him fast to death / at the hands of Prince Telemachus and his spear" (18.178–179). Just as Poseidon vents his wrath on the well-intentioned Phaeacians, in Book 13, for treating his nemesis Odysseus kindly, Athena condemns Amphinomus to the same fate as the most worthless suitors of the bunch.

Homer continues to individualize the suitors, with the seeming purpose of exposing their specific character flaws. In Book 17, for example, he gives us the most critical depiction yet of Antinous, who disgusts even the other suitors with his abuse of the disguised Odysseus. Whereas other suitors at least give the beggar food, Antinous displays nothing but contempt for the man's apparent low breeding and physically assails him; Penelope thus labels Antinous "the worst of all . . . black death itself" (17.554). Homer portrays Antinous as an ignoble noble, and Antinous's detractors often point out the disparity between the nobility of his birth and the baseness of his actions ("'Antinous, / highborn as you are . . . / that was a mean low speech!'" [17.417–419]).

The explanation for the contempt in which the others hold Antinous for mistreating Odysseus lies in the feudal structure of Homeric society, which was bound together by reciprocal obligations and responsibilities among people of different social classes. While it would be a mistake to think that the Greeks considered mistreatment of the poor an automatic sign of evil or moral deficiency, we definitely get the sense that Antinous is abusing his rank when he beats the seemingly helpless beggar. Antinous is guilty not of pure evil but of a kind of arrogance. Accordingly, the insults hurled at him accuse him not of straying from some moral code but of straying from the expectations of his noble birth.

BOOKS 19–20

SUMMARY: BOOK 19

When the suitors retire for the night, Telemachus and Odysseus remove the arms as planned. Athena lights the room for them so that they can see as they work. Telemachus tells Eurycleia that they are storing the arms to keep them from being damaged.

After they have safely disposed of the arms, Telemachus retires and Odysseus is joined by Penelope. She has come from the women's quarters to question her curious visitor. She knows that he has claimed to have met Odysseus, and she tests his honesty by asking him to describe her husband. Odysseus describes the Greek hero—himself, capturing each detail so perfectly that it reduces Penelope to tears. He then tells the story of how he met Odysseus and eventually came to Ithaca. In many respects, this story parallels those that he told to Athena and Eumaeus in Books 13 and 14, respectively, though it is identical to neither. He tells Penelope that, essentially, Odysseus had a long ordeal but is alive and freely traveling the seas, and predicts that Odysseus will be back within the month.

Penelope offers the beggar a bed to sleep in, but he is used to the floor, he says, and declines. Only reluctantly does he allow Eurycleia to wash his feet. As she is putting them in a basin of water, she notices a scar on one of his feet. She immediately recognizes it as the scar that Odysseus received when he went boar hunting with his grandfather Autolycus. She throws her arms around Odysseus, but he silences her while Athena keeps Penelope distracted so that Odysseus's secret will not be carried any further. The faithful Eurycleia recovers herself and promises to keep his secret.

Before she retires, Penelope describes to Odysseus a dream that she has had in which an eagle swoops down upon her twenty pet geese and kills them all; it then perches on her roof and, in a human voice, says that he is her husband who has just put her lovers to death. Penelope declares that she has no idea what this dream means. Rising to the challenge, Odysseus explains it to her. But Penelope decides that she is going to choose a new husband nevertheless: she will marry the first man who can shoot an arrow through the holes of twelve axes set in a line.

Summary: Book 20

Penelope and Odysseus both have trouble sleeping that night. Odysseus worries that he and Telemachus will never be able to conquer so many suitors, but Athena reassures him that through the gods all things are possible. Tormented by the loss of her husband and her commitment to remarry, Penelope wakes and prays for Artemis to kill her. Her distress wakes Odysseus, who asks Zeus for a good omen. Zeus responds with a clap of thunder, and, at once, a maid in an adjacent room is heard cursing the suitors.

As the palace springs to life the next day, Odysseus and Telemachus meet, in succession, the swineherd Eumaeus, the foul Melanthius, and Philoetius, a kindly and loyal herdsman who says that he has not yet given up hope of Odysseus's return. The suitors enter, once again plotting Telemachus's murder. Amphinomus convinces them to call it off, however, when a portent of doom appears in the form of an eagle carrying a dove in its talons. But Athena keeps the suitors antagonistic all through dinner to prevent Odysseus's anger from losing its edge. Ctesippus, a wealthy and arrogant suitor, throws a cow's hoof at Odysseus, in response to which Telemachus threatens to run him through with his sword. The suitors laugh and laugh, failing to notice that they and the walls of the room are covered in blood and that their faces have assumed a foreign, ghostly look— all of which Theoclymenus interprets as portents of inescapable doom.

ANALYSIS: BOOKS 19–20

More and more, the suitors' destruction feels inevitable. While portents earlier in the epic appear irregularly and serve primarily to keep hope alive among Odysseus's family and friends, they now occur at a feverish rate and with such obvious implications that they foreshadow the suitors' fate with increasingly grim effect. These omens are noticeably more violent than earlier ones: in Book 15, as Telemachus departs from Sparta, an eagle grasping a goose soars overhead, but the eagle flies away before killing its prey. In Penelope's dream, on the other hand, an eagle "snap[s] [the geeses'] necks and kill[s] them one and all," leaving them in "heaps" (19.607–608). Not only are there more geese-victims of vengeance—but their slaughter, which Penelope sees in her dream, is much more graphic and, hence, immediate. Additionally, Zeus's propitious thunderclap in Book 20 immediately precedes a maidservant's cursing to Zeus about the suitors. This heightening of omens reaches a grotesque climax when the suitors suddenly appear deformed and bloody as they eat their final meal in the palace.

It seems unclear whether the human participants in these events are truly responsible for their own actions. The suitors react impudently to Telemachus at the end of Book 20 in part because Athena has robbed them of their wits. She manipulates them, egging on their abuse of Odysseus in order to enrage him further. Similarly, Athena's words of encouragement to Odysseus at the beginning of Book 20 make it sound as if victory is already assured and that she, not Odysseus, will be the decisive factor. Like *The Iliad, The Odyssey* often depicts the gods arranging the future based on the outcomes of great debates on Mount Olympus: the gods lift their favorite mortals to success and ensure that their enemies are crushed, just as Athena does with Odysseus and the suitors. While the fatalism of *The Odyssey* may puzzle modern readers, it is entirely consistent with the outlook of Homeric poetry. Again, Homeric audiences would have been familiar with the poem's plot; it is Odysseus's internal struggle and consequent development that would have kept the audience riveted.

The second half of *The Odyssey* has been criticized for its long and largely uneventful account of the time that Odysseus spends disguised on his estate. Much of this length results from repetition: the suitors plot against Telemachus over and over; Odysseus has things thrown at him again and again; his ignorant servants insult him time after time; Odysseus repeats his false story about being from Crete. Some scholars argue that the second half of *The Odyssey* shows signs of multiple authorship—that it looks less like a single narrative thread than several accounts of the same story sewn together.

But Homer uses repetition quite frequently elsewhere in *The Odyssey* and *The Iliad*. Indeed, repetition is a standard feature of oral poems, which, like modern songs, rely on echoes and refrains for unity and emphasis of individual ideas. Additionally, repetition in the poem often occurs with some variation from occurrence to occurrence or with a change in context that gives repeated phrases or encounters new meaning. For instance, while the suitors hurl the same insults at Odysseus more than a few times, both his and Telemachus's reactions to them gradually change. At first, they generally respond with anger, as when, in Book 19, Odysseus launches into an extended tirade against Melantho. By the end of Book 20, however, they seem to respond with something closer to disgust or pity, as when Odysseus merely shakes his head at Melanthius's disparaging remarks. Father and son have become less reactionary, perhaps because they now accept their antagonists' arrogance as pathetic and their doom as inescapable.

The repeated observation that the beggar resembles Odysseus helps to build tension leading up to the final confrontation. Each remark about the resemblance raises the possibility that Odysseus's cover will be blown, as nearly happens in the scene with Eurycleia.

Since revelation of his identity would, of course, force Odysseus to take the actions that eventually bring about the resolution of *The Odyssey,* this repetition has the effect of bringing the audience closer and closer to the epic's climax. Homer stalls the arrival of the climax, keeping the audience tantalized.

Books 21–22

Summary: Book 21

Penelope gets Odysseus's bow out of the storeroom and announces that she will marry the suitor who can string it and then shoot an arrow through a line of twelve axes. Telemachus sets up the axes and then tries his own hand at the bow, but fails in his attempt to string it. The suitors warm and grease the bow to make it supple, but one by one they all try and fail.

Meanwhile, Odysseus follows Eumaeus and Philoetius outside. He assures himself of their loyalty and then reveals his identity to them by means of the scar on his foot. He promises to treat them as Telemachus's brothers if they fight by his side against the suitors.

When Odysseus returns, Eurymachus has the bow. He feels disgraced that he cannot string it, because he knows that this failure proves his inferiority to Odysseus. Antinous suggests that they adjourn until the next day, when they can sacrifice to Apollo, the archer god, before trying again. Odysseus, still disguised, then asks for the bow. All of the suitors complain, fearing that he will succeed. Antinous ridicules Odysseus, saying that the wine has gone to his head and that he will bring disaster upon himself, just like the legendary drunken centaur Eurytion. Telemachus takes control and orders Eumaeus to give Odysseus the bow. Needless to say, Odysseus easily strings it and sends the first arrow he grabs whistling through all twelve axes.

Summary: Book 22

Before the suitors realize what is happening, Odysseus shoots a second arrow through the throat of Antinous. The suitors are confused and believe this shooting to be an accident. Odysseus finally reveals himself, and the suitors become terrified. They have no way out, since Philoetius has locked the front door and Eumaeus has locked the doors to the women's quarters. Eurymachus tries to calm Odysseus down, insisting that Antinous was the only bad apple among them, but Odysseus announces that he will spare none of them. Eurymachus then charges Odysseus, but he is cut down by another arrow. Amphinomus is the next to fall, at the spear of Telemachus.

Telemachus gets more shields and swords from the storeroom to arm Eumaeus and Philoetius, but he forgets to lock it on his way out. Melanthius soon reaches the storeroom and gets out fresh arms for the suitors. He isn't so lucky on his second trip to the storeroom, however, as Eumaeus and Philoetius find him there, tie him up, and lock him in.

A full battle now rages in the palace hall. Athena appears disguised as Mentor and encourages Odysseus but doesn't participate immediately, preferring instead to test Odysseus's strength. Volleys of spears are exchanged, and Odysseus and his men kill several suitors while receiving only superficial wounds themselves. Finally, Athena joins the battle, which then ends swiftly. Odysseus spares only the minstrel Phemius and the herald Medon, unwilling participants in the suitors' profligacy. The priest Leodes begs unsuccessfully for mercy.

Odysseus has Eurycleia come out. She openly rejoices to see the suitors dead, but Odysseus checks her impropriety. She rounds up the disloyal servant women, who are first made to clear the corpses from the hall and wash the blood from the furniture; they are then sent outside and executed. Odysseus tells Telemachus to cut them down with a sword, but Telemachus decides to hang them—a more disgraceful death. Last of all, the traitor Melanthius is tortured and killed. After the bloodbath, Odysseus has the house fumigated.

ANALYSIS: BOOKS 21–22

The dramatic scene in which Odysseus effortlessly strings the bow is justly famous. The bow gives double meaning to the revelation scene, for the beggar's success not only implies his true identity as Odysseus but reveals his inherent superiority to the suitors. Since the bow gives Odysseus a weapon in hand, it also allows for a seamless transition to the fighting of Book 22. Finally, the bow's associations recall Odysseus's preeminence in Ithaca before the Trojan War. Homer tells us that Odysseus received the bow during a diplomatic trip to Messene, long before any of his hardships began, and that it has been seldom used since then. The bow thus recalls the good old days when there were no suitors and Odysseus's rule was unchallenged. Through his mastery of the bow, Odysseus comes full circle, once again the king and most powerful man in Ithaca.

Athena plays a less prominent role in the battle than earlier books suggest she might. Disguised as Mentor, she offers encouragement at a crucial moment, but her departure to the sidelines puts the focus squarely on Odysseus and his allies. Though she protects them from direct hits by the suitors' spears, they still receive some wounds. Melanthius's moderate success in arming the suitors occasions a rare moment of panic for Odysseus. Of course, Athena would presumably intervene if the battle were to go awry, but her reserve until the very end allows the victory to be portrayed as the work of Odysseus and Telemachus. Indeed, as two against a host of suitors, they seem to overcome remarkable odds, whereas, if Athena were to fight openly, the odds would tilt against the suitors and thus Odysseus and Telemachus's victory would be less impressive.

When the suitors do fall, Homer makes their deaths seem fitting by reminding us of the foul deeds that merited this purge. Antinous, foremost among the suitors for his impudence, falls first. Eurymachus, who earlier insults Telemachus, falls by Telemachus's spear. When Ctesippus falls, Philoetius reminds him of his abuse of Odysseus with the cow's hoof. Even Melanthius's death contains an interesting, though seemingly unrelated, echo: he suffers the same sort of humiliating and painful dismemberments as the drunk centaur that Antinous describes in Book 21.

The fighting of Book 22 is the only pitched battle in *The Odyssey,* and while it cannot help but recall *The Iliad,* which abounds in bloodshed, the description remains thoroughly Odyssean. For one thing, it maintains the comic and domestic flavor that many critics find characteristic of *The Odyssey.* The battle, for instance, occurs not on a field but in a palace with the doors locked. Additionally, some of the deaths have a kind of Gothic humor to them, as suitors like Antinous and Eurymachus trip over their dinners. The incapacitation of Melanthius in the storeroom adds comic relief, as does his castration. Although Odysseus faces some genuinely tense moments, especially when Melanthius is procuring arms for the suitors, and although the battle is, at times, quite riveting, the grandeur and significance of *The Iliad*'s famous duels are absent from this melee. After all, these are not famous heroes fighting one another but rather one famous hero warding off a bunch of freeloaders.

BOOKS 23–24

SUMMARY: BOOK 23

Eurycleia goes upstairs to call Penelope, who has slept through the entire fight. Penelope doesn't believe anything that Eurycleia says, and she remains in disbelief even when she comes downstairs and sees her husband with her own eyes. Telemachus rebukes her for not greeting Odysseus more lovingly after his long absence, but Odysseus has other problems to worry about. He has just killed all of the noble young men of Ithaca—their parents will surely be greatly distressed. He decides that he and his family will need to lay low at their farm for a while. In the meantime, a minstrel strikes up a happy song so that no passers-by will suspect what has taken place in the palace.

Penelope remains wary, afraid that a god is playing a trick on her. She orders Eurycleia to move her bridal bed, and Odysseus suddenly flares up at her that their bed is immovable, explaining how it is built from the trunk of an olive tree around which the house had been constructed. Hearing him recount these details, she knows that this man must be her husband. They get reacquainted and, afterward, Odysseus gives his wife a brief account of his wanderings. He also tells her about the trip that he must make to fulfill the prophecy of Tiresias in Book 11. The next day, he leaves with Telemachus for Laertes' orchard. He gives Penelope instructions not to leave her room or receive any visitors. Athena cloaks Odysseus and Telemachus in darkness so that no one will see them as they walk through the town.

SUMMARY: BOOK 24

The scene changes abruptly. Hermes leads the souls of the suitors, crying like bats, into Hades. Agamemnon and Achilles argue over who had the better death. Agamemnon describes Achilles' funeral in detail. They see the suitors coming in and ask how so many noble young men met their end. The suitor Amphimedon, whom Agamemnon knew in life, gives a brief account of their ruin, pinning most of the blame on Penelope and her indecision. Agamemnon contrasts the constancy of Penelope with the treachery of Clytemnestra.

Back in Ithaca, Odysseus travels to Laertes' farm. He sends his servants into the house so that he can be alone with his father in the gardens. Odysseus finds that Laertes has aged prematurely out of grief for his son and wife. He doesn't recognize Odysseus, and

Odysseus doesn't immediately reveal himself, pretending instead that he is someone who once knew and befriended Odysseus. But when Laertes begins to cry at the memory of Odysseus, Odysseus throws his arms around Laertes and kisses him. He proves his identity with the scar and with his memories of the fruit trees that Laertes gave him when he was a little boy. He tells Laertes how he has avenged himself upon the suitors.

Laertes and Odysseus have lunch together. Dolius, the father of Melanthius and Melantho, joins them. While they eat, the goddess Rumor flies through the city spreading the news of the massacre at the palace. The parents of the suitors hold an assembly at which they assess how to respond. Halitherses, the elder prophet, argues that the suitors merely got what they deserved for their wickedness, but Eupithes, Antinous's father, encourages the parents to seek revenge on Odysseus. Their small army tracks Odysseus to Laertes' house, but Athena, disguised again as Mentor, decides to put a stop to the violence. Antinous's father is the only one killed, felled by one of Laertes' spears. Athena makes the Ithacans forget the massacre of their children and recognize Odysseus as king. Peace is thus restored.

ANALYSIS: BOOKS 23–24

The scene in which Penelope tests her husband's knowledge of the bed neatly brings together several ideas that the epic has touched on before. This subtle test reveals Penelope's clever side—the side we have seen in her ploy to use a never-to-be-finished burial shroud to put off remarriage for four years. This test not only admits Odysseus to Penelope's arms but also sheds some light on why their love for each other is so natural in the first place. They are united by the commonality of their minds, by their love of scheming, testing, and outmaneuvering. They are kindred spirits because they are kindred wits. None of the suitors could ever replace Odysseus, just as Circe or Calypso could never replace Penelope. Literally and metaphorically, no one can move their wedding bed.

What follows this scene has troubled Homeric scholars for over two thousand years. Some believe that the epic originally ended with Odysseus and Penelope returning at last together to their marriage bed. The end of this scene gives the story nice closure, while the scenes that follow seem un-Homeric. The bat metaphor at the beginning of Book 24 is unusual, as most Homeric metaphors exploit bright, pastoral imagery. The description of the suitors being led into the underworld is even more troubling, since it deviates from the Homeric principle that only the soul of a properly buried body can enter Hades. Book 11 bears out this principle, as Elpenor petitions Odysseus for a proper burial, unable otherwise to gain entrance to the underworld.

The early ending theory also rests on a subjective evaluation of the quality of the present ending. To many, Book 24 seems inferior to the rest of *The Odyssey*. The conversation between Achilles and Agamemnon has little point or relevance to the story; the conversation between Odysseus and Laertes is clumsy; Odysseus's revelation to his father of his identity seems anticlimactic after the tension that he creates with his disguise. Furthermore, the lunch with Dolius ends without exploring or even acknowledging the obvious tension that should exist between Dolius and Odysseus since Odysseus has murdered Dolius's two children. Halitherses' speech in the assembly piles on blame gratuitously and without sophistication, and Athena's tacit support for the exclusive murder of Antinous's father—a character introduced only a few lines earlier—is bizarre.

At the same time, ending the epic with Odysseus and Penelope's first night together leaves too many threads hanging. The suitors' families will doubtless be enraged when they discover what has happened to their children, as Odysseus himself predicts. Something must be done to appease or stop them, but the earlier ending would leave this problem unaddressed. It would also leave Odysseus in the odd position of having revealed his identity to all of his loved ones (including Eurycleia) except his own father, even though Laertes' grief at Odysseus's absence is rivaled only by that of Odysseus's deceased mother. It is perhaps fitting, then, for Homer's audience— the gods-worshipping warrior culture of Greece—that an epic so marked by divine intervention should end with Athena restoring peace and urging Odysseus not to "court the rage of Zeus who rules the world!" (24.597).

Important Quotations Explained

1. Sing to me of the man, Muse, the man of twists and turns
driven time and again off course, once he had plundered
the hallowed heights of Troy.
Many cities of men he saw and learned their minds,
many pains he suffered, heartsick on the open sea,
fighting to save his life and bring his comrades home.
But he could not save them from disaster, hard as he strove—
the recklessness of their own ways destroyed them all,
the blind fools, they devoured the cattle of the Sun
and the Sungod blotted out the day of their return.
Launch out on his story, Muse, daughter of Zeus,
start from where you will—sing for our time too.

With these words *The Odyssey* begins. The poet asks for inspiration from the Muse and imagines her singing through him. An ancient epic poem states at the outset, in capsule form, the subject of the work to follow, and this epic is no exception. *The Odyssey* announces its subject matter in a different fashion from *The Iliad*. Whereas Homer's first epic treats Achilles' rage, this one focuses on a "man of twists and turns." It chronicles not battles, the stuff of Achilles' brief life, but a long journey through "[m]any cities" and "many pains," the kind of test worthy of a resourceful hero like Odysseus. The opening lines foreshadow how the epic will end—with all of Odysseus's men dead except Odysseus himself—and provide a reason for these deaths: the recklessness and blindness of his crew, who do not realize that by slaughtering the Sun's cattle they seal their own dooms. The opening leaves unmentioned many other temptations the Achaeans will face and says nothing of the situation in Ithaca, which consumes nearly half the epic. It treats the subject matter of the epic in an abbreviated form but captures the themes those subjects will explore. As Knox notes in the introduction to the Fagles translation, in *The Odyssey*, in contrast to *The Iliad*, the Muse is asked to choose where to begin. Giving the Muse this freedom prepares us for the more complex narrative structure of *The Odyssey*, which relies on flashbacks as it moves through the many settings of the hero's ten-year journey.

2.   So then,
          royal son of Laertes, Odysseus, man of exploits,
          still eager to leave at once and hurry back
          to your own home, your beloved native land?
          Good luck to you, even so. Farewell!
          But if you only knew, down deep, what pains
          are fated to fill your cup before you reach that shore,
          you'd stay right here, preside in our house with me
          and be immortal. Much as you long to see your wife,
          the one you pine for all your days . . .

Calypso makes this final plea to Odysseus in Book 5, begging him to stay with her, and her temptation trumps all those Odysseus has seen before (5.223–232). She not only promises to save him from having to face future woes but to give him what no other human character in *The Odyssey* has: immortality. But Odysseus is not interested. All he wants is his home and wife, even though he admits in ensuing lines that Penelope cannot match Calypso in beauty. Calypso's plea embodies the tension in Odysseus's journey. He wants to see his wife and home again, but he also presumably wants all the tempting things Calypso has to offer. That she asks him one last time whether he wants to leave suggests (even if the question is just rhetorical) that she knows her offer is tempting, but the fact that Odysseus can refuse it and embrace all the "pains" she foretells shows how compelling his homecoming really is.

QUOTATIONS

3.   "But you, Achilles,
      there's not a man in the world more blest than you—
      there never has been, never will be one.
      Time was, when you were alive, we Argives
      honored you as a god, and now down here, I see,
      you lord it over the dead in all your power.
      So grieve no more at dying, great Achilles."

      I reassured the ghost, but he broke out, protesting,
      "No winning words about death to me, shining Odysseus!
      By god, I'd rather slave on earth for another man—
      some dirt-poor tenant farmer who scrapes to keep alive—
      than rule down here over all the breathless dead."

This exchange comes as part of the conversation between Achilles and Odysseus when the latter journeys to the underworld in Book 11 (11.547–558). (The entire event is told as a flashback to the Phaeacians by Odysseus.) The heroes muse on the differences between the two worlds they now inhabit, and each finds the grass greener on the other side. Odysseus envies Achilles' strength and the glory that it won him; Achilles envies Odysseus for being alive. The differences reflect the change in outlook between *The Iliad* and *The Odyssey*. The first epic celebrates the glory (*kleos*) that comes from winning battles, and the mighty Achilles is naturally the focus. In *The Odyssey*, whose focus is the wily Odysseus, that earlier outlook is implicitly criticized. Achilles did win great glory, but it came at the cost of an early death, and he would do anything now to return to earth and live a life without glory. His indignant reply, "No winning words about death to me," suggests that he does not believe Odysseus is speaking sincerely, but Odysseus means what he says and thus needs a warning like this so badly. Like other Greek heroes, Odysseus has a glory-loving streak. He too would like to be "honored . . . as a god," but he must not lose his wits in his pursuit of glory.

4.   Of all that breathes and crawls across the earth,
       our mother earth breeds nothing feebler than a man.
       So long as the gods grant him power, spring in his knees,
       he thinks he will never suffer affliction down the years.
       But then, when the happy gods bring on the long hard times,
       bear them he must, against his will, and steel his heart.
       Our lives, our mood and mind as we pass across the earth,
       turn as the days turn . . .

Odysseus utters these words to the suitor Amphinomus shortly
after defeating the "Beggar-King" Irus in Book 18 (18.150–157).
Odysseus is himself in disguise as beggar, and his words here help
maintain that cover. According to the story he has told, he once was
a great warrior, plundering faraway lands, until one day he was captured. On one level, his words here reinforce those lies. The fatalism
and helplessness he expresses—that a man only prospers while "the
gods grant him power"—were frequently expressed sentiments of
the Ancient Greek outlook, but they seem especially natural coming
from a onetime king who has descended to the status of a beggar.
Who better to comment on life's reversals than someone who has
experienced them firsthand?

The words have additional meaning, however, for both Amphinomus and Odysseus. For Amphinomus, they foreshadow death.
He is plundering the land of others, living a careless life, much as the
beggar once did, but he too is a feeble man, and he is destined for a
fall. The words are a prophecy to Amphinomus, and a warning; he
does not miss their meaning, as he walks away "fraught with grave
forebodings" (18.176). For Odysseus, on the other hand, the words
do not foretell the future but recount the past and, perhaps, explain
the lesson it has taught him. At the hour of his greatest triumph, the
beginning of his *nostos* ("homeward journey") from the city he had
helped sack, his life "turn[ed]" and the gods began his suffering. He
endured only by "steel[ing] his heart," and he knows now that at
such moments that is all that can be done.

5.   Just as I
    have come from afar, creating pain for many—
    men and women across the good green earth—
    so let his name be Odysseus . . .
    the Son of Pain, a name he'll earn in full.

With these words in the middle of Book 19, Homer explains the origin of Odysseus's name (19.460–464). They are actually spoken by his grandfather Autolycus, who named the hero when he was an infant. The name implies that pain, like dark hair or some other physical attribute, is in some way in his blood, which may be true in two senses. First, as Autolycus happily brags, Odysseus is the grandson of someone who has created pain for many, and he might be expected to inherit this quality and grow up like his grandfather. Pain is part of his makeup because, like some kind of physical attribute, he is destined to live with it from birth. The name recognizes that pain will be a constant in his life. He may not always be on the receiving end of it (*The Odyssey* provides at least as many examples of Odysseus giving pain to others as feeling its sting himself), but it will always be there, like an extension of his body. From minor incidents like the goring that gives him his scar—which happens, not coincidentally, while he is on a hunting trip with his grandfather—to the massacre of the suitors, *The Odyssey* suggests that Odysseus has indeed earned his name "in full."

QUOTATIONS

KEY FACTS

FULL TITLE
The Odyssey

AUTHOR
Homer; some critics argue for multiple authorship

TYPE OF WORK
Poem

GENRE
Epic

LANGUAGE
Ancient Greek (Ionic dialect mixed with archaic forms and other dialects)

TIME AND PLACE WRITTEN
Unknown, but probably mainland Greece, approximately 700 B.C.E.

DATE OF FIRST PUBLICATION
Unknown

NARRATOR
The poet, who invokes the assistance of the Muse; Odysseus narrates Books 9–12.

POINT OF VIEW
The narrator speaks in the third person and is omniscient. He frequently offers insight into the thoughts and feelings of even minor characters, gods and mortals alike; Odysseus narrates Books 9–12 in the first person. Odysseus freely gives inferences about the thoughts and feelings of other characters.

TONE
Celebratory and nostalgic; the poet views the times in which the action is set as glorious and larger than life.

TENSE
Past; large portions of the poem (especially Books 9–12) are narrated in flashbacks.

SETTING (TIME)

Bronze Age (approximately twelfth century B.C.E.); *The Odyssey* begins where *The Iliad* ends and covers the ten years after the fall of Troy.

SETTING (PLACE)

Odysseus's wanderings cover the Aegean and surrounding seas and eventually end in Ithaca, in northwestern Greece; Telemachus travels from Ithaca to southern Greece.

PROTAGONIST

Odysseus

MAJOR CONFLICT

Odysseus must return home and vanquish the suitors who threaten his estate; Telemachus must mature and secure his own reputation in Greek society.

RISING ACTION

The return of Odysseus to Ithaca; the return of Telemachus to Ithaca; their entrance into the palace; the abuse Odysseus receives; the various omens; the hiding of the arms and locking of the palace doors; Penelope's challenge to the suitors; the stringing of the bow

CLIMAX

The beginning of Book 22, when the beggar in the palace reveals his true identity as Odysseus

FALLING ACTION

Odysseus and Telemachus fight and kill the suitors; they put to death the suitors' allies among the palace servants.

THEMES

The power of cunning over strength; the pitfalls of temptation; the tension between goals and obstacles; the misery of separation; maturation as a journey

MOTIFS

Disguises; storytelling; seductresses

SYMBOLS

Food; the wedding bed; the great bow; symbols of temptation (Circe, the lotus, the Sirens' song, the cattle of the Sun)

FORESHADOWING

Agamemnon's fate at the hands of his wife and his vindication by his son foreshadow the domestic troubles and triumphs Odysseus faces when he returns to Ithaca; Odysseus is nearly recognized by his wife and servants several times in Books 18–19, foreshadowing the revelation of his identity in Book 22.

KEY FACTS

STUDY QUESTIONS

1. *How does Homer portray the relationship between gods and men in* THE ODYSSEY? *What roles do the gods play in human life? How does this portrayal differ from that found in* THE ILIAD?

In *The Iliad,* the gods relate to human beings either as external powers that influence the lives of mortals from without, as when Apollo unleashes plague upon the Achaeans, or from within, as when Aphrodite incites Helen to make love to Paris or when Athena gives Diomedes courage in battle. In *The Odyssey,* the gods are often much less grand. They function more as spiritual guides and supporters for their human subjects, sometimes assuming mortal disguises in order to do so. The actions of the gods sometimes remain otherworldly, as when Poseidon decides to wreck the ship of the Phaeacians, but generally they grant direct aid to particular individuals. In a sense, the change in the behavior of the gods is wholly appropriate to the shift in focus between the two epics. *The Iliad* depicts a violent and glorious war, and the gods act as frighteningly powerful, supernatural forces. *The Odyssey,* in contrast, chronicles a long journey, and the gods frequently act to guide and advise the wandering hero.

2. *In what ways does Odysseus develop as a character during the course of the narrative? Does he develop at all?*

Odysseus does not change remarkably during the course of the narrative, especially in comparison to Telemachus, who undergoes a rite of passage from naive adolescence to manhood. Odysseus, already a famed soldier at the beginning of *The Iliad,* continues his role as the most intelligent and courageous of all the Achaean heroes. But this is not to say that Odysseus exhibits no signs of growth. Just as Achilles is confronted in *The Iliad* with the problem of balancing his honor with his pride, Odysseus repeatedly faces situations in which self-restraint and humility must check bravado and glory-seeking. In his early adventures, he often fails these tests, as when he boastfully taunts Polyphemus, enflaming Poseidon.

As the epic progresses, Odysseus becomes increasingly capable of judging when it is wise to reveal himself and when it is appropriate to exult in his accomplishments. At Scheria, he prudently waits until late in his visit before declaring his identity to the king and queen. By the time he reaches Ithaca, he can endure the insults of the suitors for the better part of two days. The ability to hold his passions and pride in check make his swift and total revenge upon the suitors possible. Odysseus's internal conflict is not nearly as consuming as that of Achilles in *The Iliad,* making up a relatively small part of his overall journey, but he too is a wiser and stronger man at the end of his epic.

3. *One of the most important cultural values in* The Odyssey *is that of* xenia, *a Greek concept encompassing the generosity and courtesy shown to those who are far from home. Why might hospitality have held more significance in Homer's time than it does in today's world? How is hospitality established as a key value in the epic?*

Odysseus's journey takes place in a world in which vast swaths of uninhabited land separate human civilizations. Traveling between those settlements involves facing both natural and supernatural perils, as well as logistical problems like shortages in provisions. The code of hospitality operates as a linchpin that allows individuals such as Odysseus to undertake these kinds of journeys at all. It is a set of reciprocal expectations and obligations that not only mitigate the privations of travel but forge and reinforce bonds of friendship and goodwill. Not surprisingly, *The Odyssey* doles out harsh punishments to those who do not respect this sacred social code. Polyphemus, the suitors, and the Achaean soldiers at Ismarus all suffer for violating it. By the same token, individuals such as Eumaeus and the Phaeacian royalty prove their worth to Odysseus by showering him with selfless generosity and kindness. Within *The Odyssey,* adherence to the code functions as a kind of imperfect currency. If one acts in accordance with the rules, one will generally, but not always, be rewarded.

How to Write
Literary Analysis

The Literary Essay: A Step-by-Step Guide

When you read for pleasure, your only goal is enjoyment. You might find yourself reading to get caught up in an exciting story, to learn about an interesting time or place, or just to pass time. Maybe you're looking for inspiration, guidance, or a reflection of your own life. There are as many different, valid ways of reading a book as there are books in the world.

When you read a work of literature in an English class, however, you're being asked to read in a special way: you're being asked to perform *literary analysis*. To analyze something means to break it down into smaller parts and then examine how those parts work, both individually and together. Literary analysis involves examining all the parts of a novel, play, short story, or poem—elements such as character, setting, tone, and imagery—and thinking about how the author uses those elements to create certain effects.

A literary essay isn't a book review: you're not being asked whether or not you liked a book or whether you'd recommend it to another reader. A literary essay also isn't like the kind of book report you wrote when you were younger, where your teacher wanted you to summarize the book's action. A high school- or college-level literary essay asks, "How does this piece of literature actually work?" "How does it do what it does?" and, "Why might the author have made the choices he or she did?"

The Seven Steps

No one is born knowing how to analyze literature; it's a skill you learn and a process you can master. As you gain more practice with this kind of thinking and writing, you'll be able to craft a method that works best for you. But until then, here are seven basic steps to writing a well-constructed literary essay:

 1. Ask questions
 2. Collect evidence
 3. Construct a thesis

4. Develop and organize arguments
5. Write the introduction
6. Write the body paragraphs
7. Write the conclusion

---

1. ASK QUESTIONS

When you're assigned a literary essay in class, your teacher will often provide you with a list of writing prompts. Lucky you! Now all you have to do is choose one. Do yourself a favor and pick a topic that interests you. You'll have a much better (not to mention easier) time if you start off with something you enjoy thinking about. If you are asked to come up with a topic by yourself, though, you might start to feel a little panicked. Maybe you have too many ideas—or none at all. Don't worry. Take a deep breath and start by asking yourself these questions:

- **What struck you?** Did a particular image, line, or scene linger in your mind for a long time? If it fascinated you, chances are you can draw on it to write a fascinating essay.

- **What confused you?** Maybe you were surprised to see a character act in a certain way, or maybe you didn't understand why the book ended the way it did. Confusing moments in a work of literature are like a loose thread in a sweater: if you pull on it, you can unravel the entire thing. Ask yourself why the author chose to write about that character or scene the way he or she did and you might tap into some important insights about the work as a whole.

- **Did you notice any patterns?** Is there a phrase that the main character uses constantly or an image that repeats throughout the book? If you can figure out how that pattern weaves through the work and what the significance of that pattern is, you've almost got your entire essay mapped out.

- **Did you notice any contradictions or ironies?** Great works of literature are complex; great literary essays recognize and explain those complexities. Maybe the title (*Happy Days*) totally disagrees with the book's subject matter (hungry orphans dying in the woods). Maybe the main character acts one way around his family and a completely different way around his friends and associates. If you can find a way to explain a work's contradictory elements, you've got the seeds of a great essay.

At this point, you don't need to know exactly what you're going to say about your topic; you just need a place to begin your exploration. You can help direct your reading and brainstorming by formulating your topic as a *question,* which you'll then try to answer in your essay. The best questions invite critical debates and discussions, not just a rehashing of the summary. Remember, you're looking for something you can *prove or argue* based on evidence you find in the text. Finally, remember to keep the scope of your question in mind: is this a topic you can adequately address within the word or page limit you've been given? Conversely, is this a topic big enough to fill the required length?

GOOD QUESTIONS

"Are Romeo and Juliet's parents responsible for the deaths of their children?"

"Why do pigs keep showing up in LORD OF THE FLIES*?"*

"Are Dr. Frankenstein and his monster alike? How?"

BAD QUESTIONS

"What happens to Scout in TO KILL A MOCKINGBIRD*?"*

"What do the other characters in JULIUS CAESAR *think about Caesar?"*

"How does Hester Prynne in THE SCARLET LETTER *remind me of my sister?"*

---

2. COLLECT EVIDENCE

Once you know what question you want to answer, it's time to scour the book for things that will help you answer the question. Don't worry if you don't know what you want to say yet—right now you're just collecting ideas and material and letting it all percolate. Keep track of passages, symbols, images, or scenes that deal with your topic. Eventually, you'll start making connections between these examples and your thesis will emerge.

Here's a brief summary of the various parts that compose each and every work of literature. These are the elements that you will analyze in your essay, and which you will offer as evidence to support your arguments. For more on the parts of literary works, see the Glossary of Literary Terms at the end of this section.

LITERARY ANALYSIS

ELEMENTS OF STORY   These are the *what*s of the work—what happens, where it happens, and to whom it happens.

- **Plot:** All of the events and actions of the work.

- **Character:** The people who act and are acted upon in a literary work. The main character of a work is known as the *protagonist.*

- **Conflict:** The central tension in the work. In most cases, the protagonist wants something, while opposing forces (antagonists) hinder the protagonist's progress.

- **Setting:** When and where the work takes place. Elements of setting include location, time period, time of day, weather, social atmosphere, and economic conditions.

- **Narrator:** The person telling the story. The narrator may straightforwardly report what happens, convey the subjective opinions and perceptions of one or more characters, or provide commentary and opinion in his or her own voice.

- **Themes:** The main idea or message of the work—usually an abstract idea about people, society, or life in general. A work may have many themes, which may be in tension with one another.

ELEMENTS OF STYLE   These are the *how*s—how the characters speak, how the story is constructed, and how language is used throughout the work.

- **Structure and organization:** How the parts of the work are assembled. Some novels are narrated in a linear, chronological fashion, while others skip around in time. Some plays follow a traditional three- or five-act structure, while others are a series of loosely connected scenes. Some authors deliberately leave gaps in their works, leaving readers to puzzle out the missing information. A work's structure and organization can tell you a lot about the kind of message it wants to convey.

- **Point of view:** The perspective from which a story is told. In *first-person point of view,* the narrator involves him or herself in the story. ("I went to the store"; "We watched in horror as the bird slammed into the window.") A first-person narrator is usually the protagonist of the work, but not always. In *third-person point of view,* the narrator does not participate in the story. A third-person narrator may closely follow a specific character, recounting that individual character's thoughts or experiences, or it may be what we call an *omniscient* narrator. Omniscient narrators see and know all: they can witness any event in any time or place and are privy to the inner thoughts and feelings of all characters. Remember that the narrator and the author are not the same thing!

- **Diction:** Word choice. Whether a character uses dry, clinical language or flowery prose with lots of exclamation points can tell you a lot about his or her attitude and personality.

- **Syntax:** Word order and sentence construction. Syntax is a crucial part of establishing an author's narrative voice. Ernest Hemingway, for example, is known for writing in very short, straightforward sentences, while James Joyce characteristically wrote in long, incredibly complicated lines.

- **Tone:** The mood or feeling of the text. Diction and syntax often contribute to the tone of a work. A novel written in short, clipped sentences that use small, simple words might feel brusque, cold, or matter-of-fact.

- **Imagery:** Language that appeals to the senses, representing things that can be seen, smelled, heard, tasted, or touched.

- **Figurative language:** Language that is not meant to be interpreted literally. The most common types of figurative language are *metaphors* and *similes,* which compare two unlike things in order to suggest a similarity between them— for example, "All the world's a stage," or "The moon is like a ball of green cheese." (Metaphors say one thing *is* another thing; similes claim that one thing is *like* another thing.)

3. Construct a Thesis

When you've examined all the evidence you've collected and know how you want to answer the question, it's time to write your thesis statement. A *thesis* is a claim about a work of literature that needs to be supported by evidence and arguments. The thesis statement is the heart of the literary essay, and the bulk of your paper will be spent trying to prove this claim. A good thesis will be:

- **Arguable.** "*The Great Gatsby* describes New York society in the 1920s" isn't a thesis—it's a fact.

- **Provable through textual evidence.** "*Hamlet* is a confusing but ultimately very well-written play" is a weak thesis because it offers the writer's personal opinion about the book. Yes, it's arguable, but it's not a claim that can be proved or supported with examples taken from the play itself.

- **Surprising.** "Both George and Lenny change a great deal in *Of Mice and Men*" is a weak thesis because it's obvious. A really strong thesis will argue for a reading of the text that is not immediately apparent.

- **Specific.** "Dr. Frankenstein's monster tells us a lot about the human condition" is *almost* a really great thesis statement, but it's still too vague. What does the writer mean by "a lot"? *How* does the monster tell us so much about the human condition?

GOOD THESIS STATEMENTS

Question: In *Romeo and Juliet*, which is more powerful in shaping the lovers' story: fate or foolishness?

Thesis: "Though Shakespeare defines Romeo and Juliet as 'star-crossed lovers' and images of stars and planets appear throughout the play, a closer examination of that celestial imagery reveals that the stars are merely witnesses to the characters' foolish activities and not the causes themselves."

Question: How does the bell jar function as a symbol in Sylvia Plath's *The Bell Jar*?

Thesis: "A bell jar is a bell-shaped glass that has three basic uses: to hold a specimen for observation, to contain gases, and to maintain a vacuum. The bell jar appears in each of these capacities in *The Bell Jar*, Plath's semi-autobiographical novel, and each appearance marks a different stage in Esther's mental breakdown."

Question: Would Piggy in *The Lord of the Flies* make a good island leader if he were given the chance?

Thesis: "Though the intelligent, rational, and innovative Piggy has the mental characteristics of a good leader, he ultimately lacks the social skills necessary to be an effective one. Golding emphasizes this point by giving Piggy a foil in the charismatic Jack, whose magnetic personality allows him to capture and wield power effectively, if not always wisely."

4. DEVELOP AND ORGANIZE ARGUMENTS

The reasons and examples that support your thesis will form the middle paragraphs of your essay. Since you can't really write your thesis statement until you know how you'll structure your argument, you'll probably end up working on steps 3 and 4 at the same time.

There's no single method of argumentation that will work in every context. One essay prompt might ask you to compare and contrast two characters, while another asks you to trace an image through a given work of literature. These questions require different kinds of answers and therefore different kinds of arguments. Below, we'll discuss three common kinds of essay prompts and some strategies for constructing a solid, well-argued case.

TYPES OF LITERARY ESSAYS

- **Compare and contrast**

  Compare and contrast the characters of Huck and Jim in THE ADVENTURES OF HUCKLEBERRY FINN.

  Chances are you've written this kind of essay before. In an academic literary context, you'll organize your arguments the same way you would in any other class. You can either go *subject by subject* or *point by point*. In the former, you'll discuss one character first and then the second. In the latter, you'll choose several traits (attitude toward life, social status, images and metaphors associated with the character) and devote a paragraph to each. You may want to use a mix of these two approaches—for example, you may want to spend a paragraph a piece broadly sketching Huck's and Jim's personalities before transitioning into a paragraph or two that describes a few key points of comparison. This can be a highly effective strategy if you want to make a counterintuitive argument—that, despite seeming to be totally different, the two objects being compared are actually similar in a very important way (or vice versa). Remember that your essay should reveal something fresh or unexpected about the text, so think beyond the obvious parallels and differences.

- **Trace**

  Choose an image—for example, birds, knives, or eyes—and trace that image throughout MACBETH.

  Sounds pretty easy, right? All you need to do is read the play, underline every appearance of a knife in *Macbeth*, and then list them in your essay in the order they appear, right? Well, not exactly. Your teacher doesn't want a simple catalog of examples. He or she wants to see you make *connections* between those examples—that's the difference between summarizing and analyzing. In the *Macbeth* example above, think about the different contexts in which knives appear in the play and to what effect. In *Macbeth,* there are real knives and imagined knives; knives that kill and knives that simply threaten. Categorize and classify your examples to give them some order. Finally, always keep the overall effect in mind. After you choose and analyze your examples, you should come to some greater understanding about the work, as well as your chosen image, symbol, or phrase's role in developing the major themes and stylistic strategies of that work.

- **Debate**

  Is the society depicted in 1984 good for its citizens?

  In this kind of essay, you're being asked to debate a moral, ethical, or aesthetic issue regarding the work. You might be asked to judge a character or group of characters (*Is Caesar responsible for his own demise?*) or the work itself (*Is* JANE EYRE *a feminist novel?*). For this kind of essay, there are two important points to keep in mind. First, don't simply base your arguments on your personal feelings and reactions. Every literary essay expects you to read and analyze the work, so search for evidence in the text. What do characters in *1984* have to say about the government of Oceania? What images does Orwell use that might give you a hint about his attitude toward the government? As in any debate, you also need to make sure that you define all the necessary terms before you begin to argue your case. What does it mean to be a "good" society? What makes a novel "feminist"? You should define your terms right up front, in the first paragraph after your introduction.

  Second, remember that strong literary essays make contrary and surprising arguments. Try to think outside the box. In the *1984* example above, it seems like the obvious answer would be no, the totalitarian society depicted in Orwell's novel is *not* good for its citizens. But can you think of any arguments for the opposite side? Even if your final assertion is that the novel depicts a cruel, repressive, and therefore harmful society, acknowledging and responding to the counterargument will strengthen your overall case.

5. WRITE THE INTRODUCTION

Your introduction sets up the entire essay. It's where you present your topic and articulate the particular issues and questions you'll be addressing. It's also where you, as the writer, introduce yourself to your readers. A persuasive literary essay immediately establishes its writer as a knowledgeable, authoritative figure.

An introduction can vary in length depending on the overall length of the essay, but in a traditional five-paragraph essay it should be no longer than one paragraph. However long it is, your introduction needs to:

- **Provide any necessary context.** Your introduction should situate the reader and let him or her know what to expect. What book are you discussing? Which characters? What topic will you be addressing?

- **Answer the "So what?" question.** Why is this topic important, and why is your particular position on the topic noteworthy? Ideally, your introduction should pique the reader's interest by suggesting how your argument is surprising or otherwise counterintuitive. Literary essays make unexpected connections and reveal less-than-obvious truths.

- **Present your thesis.** This usually happens at or very near the end of your introduction.

- **Indicate the shape of the essay to come.** Your reader should finish reading your introduction with a good sense of the scope of your essay as well as the path you'll take toward proving your thesis. You don't need to spell out every step, but you do need to suggest the organizational pattern you'll be using.

Your introduction should not:

- **Be vague.** Beware of the two killer words in literary analysis: *interesting* and *important*. Of course the work, question, or example is interesting and important—that's why you're writing about it!

- **Open with any grandiose assertions.** Many student readers think that beginning their essays with a flamboyant statement such as, "Since the dawn of time, writers have been fascinated with the topic of free will," makes them sound important and commanding. You know what? It actually sounds pretty amateurish.

- **Wildly praise the work.** Another typical mistake student writers make is extolling the work or author. Your teacher doesn't need to be told that "Shakespeare is perhaps the greatest writer in the English language." You can mention a work's reputation in passing—by referring to *The Adventures of Huckleberry Finn* as "Mark Twain's enduring classic," for example—but don't make a point of bringing it up unless that reputation is key to your argument.

- **Go off-topic.** Keep your introduction streamlined and to the point. Don't feel the need to throw in all kinds of bells and whistles in order to impress your reader—just get to the point as quickly as you can, without skimping on any of the required steps.

---

6. WRITE THE BODY PARAGRAPHS

Once you've written your introduction, you'll take the arguments you developed in step 4 and turn them into your body paragraphs. The organization of this middle section of your essay will largely be determined by the argumentative strategy you use, but no matter how you arrange your thoughts, your body paragraphs need to do the following:

- **Begin with a strong topic sentence.** Topic sentences are like signs on a highway: they tell the reader where they are and where they're going. A good topic sentence not only alerts readers to what issue will be discussed in the following paragraph but also gives them a sense of what argument will be made *about* that issue. "Rumor and gossip play an important role in *The Crucible*" isn't a strong topic sentence because it doesn't tell us very much. "The community's constant gossiping creates an environment that allows false accusations to flourish" is a much stronger topic sentence— it not only tells us *what* the paragraph will discuss (gossip) but *how* the paragraph will discuss the topic (by showing how gossip creates a set of conditions that leads to the play's climactic action).

- **Fully and completely develop a single thought.** Don't skip around in your paragraph or try to stuff in too much material. Body paragraphs are like bricks: each individual one needs to be strong and sturdy or the entire structure will collapse. Make sure you have really proven your point before moving on to the next one.

- **Use transitions effectively.** Good literary essay writers know that each paragraph must be clearly and strongly linked to the material around it. Think of each paragraph as a response to the one that precedes it. Use transition words and phrases such as *however, similarly, on the contrary, therefore,* and *furthermore* to indicate what kind of response you're making.

---

7. WRITE THE CONCLUSION

Just as you used the introduction to ground your readers in the topic before providing your thesis, you'll use the conclusion to quickly summarize the specifics learned thus far and then hint at the broader implications of your topic. A good conclusion will:

- **Do more than simply restate the thesis.** If your thesis argued that *The Catcher in the Rye* can be read as a Christian allegory, don't simply end your essay by saying, "And that is why *The Catcher in the Rye* can be read as a Christian allegory." If you've constructed your arguments well, this kind of statement will just be redundant.

- **Synthesize the arguments, not summarize them.** Similarly, don't repeat the details of your body paragraphs in your conclusion. The reader has already read your essay, and chances are it's not so long that they've forgotten all your points by now.

- **Revisit the "So what?" question.** In your introduction, you made a case for why your topic and position are important. You should close your essay with the same sort of gesture. What do your readers know now that they didn't know before? How will that knowledge help them better appreciate or understand the work overall?

- **Move from the specific to the general.** Your essay has most likely treated a very specific element of the work—a single character, a small set of images, or a particular passage. In your conclusion, try to show how this narrow discussion has wider implications for the work overall. If your essay on *To Kill a Mockingbird* focused on the character of Boo Radley, for example, you might want to include a bit in your conclusion about how he fits into the novel's larger message about childhood, innocence, or family life.

- **Stay relevant.** Your conclusion should suggest new directions of thought, but it shouldn't be treated as an opportunity to pad your essay with all the extra, interesting ideas you came up with during your brainstorming sessions but couldn't fit into the essay proper. Don't attempt to stuff in unrelated queries or too many abstract thoughts.

- **Avoid making overblown closing statements.** A conclusion should open up your highly specific, focused discussion, but it should do so without drawing a sweeping lesson about life or human nature. Making such observations may be part of the point of reading, but it's almost always a mistake in essays, where these observations tend to sound overly dramatic or simply silly.

A+ ESSAY CHECKLIST

Congratulations! If you've followed all the steps we've outlined above, you should have a solid literary essay to show for all your efforts. What if you've got your sights set on an A+? To write the kind of superlative essay that will be rewarded with a perfect grade, keep the following rubric in mind. These are the qualities that teachers expect to see in a truly A+ essay. How does yours stack up?

- ✓ Demonstrates a thorough understanding of the book
- ✓ Presents an original, compelling argument
- ✓ Thoughtfully analyzes the text's formal elements
- ✓ Uses appropriate and insightful examples
- ✓ Structures ideas in a logical and progressive order
- ✓ Demonstrates a mastery of sentence construction, transitions, grammar, spelling, and word choice

LITERARY ANALYSIS

Suggested Essay Topics

1. *What is the role of family in* The Odyssey? *What values characterize the relationship between fathers and sons? You may wish to compare and contrast some of the father and son pairs in the epic (Odysseus and Telemachus, Laertes and Odysseus, Poseidon and Polyphemus, Nestor and Pisistratus, Eupithes and Antinous). How does Homer portray the idea of continuity between generations?*

2. *What is the role of women in* The Odyssey? *Focusing especially on Penelope, Calypso, or Anticleia, discuss how women are portrayed in this epic.*

3. *Compare and contrast Telemachus's journey with that of Odysseus. How does the younger man's experience enable him to grow as a character? What role does Athena play in his success?*

A+ Student Essay

> Looking at Odysseus's narrative in Books 9 through 12,
> think about the techniques Homer uses to portray the
> magical and fantastical aspects of Odysseus's adventures.
> How does he handle what we might call special effects?
> That is, how does he make his monsters fearsome, his
> goddesses stunning, the dangers frightening, etc.?

In Books 9 through 12, Odysseus relates a series of thrilling and colorful adventures. As in a successful horror movie, the spine-tingling elements and vivid characters are effective not simply on their own terms, but because of their careful deployment at just the right moment in the narrative. Two key narrative choices are made in these books of *The Odyssey:* Homer hands the storytelling reins over to Odysseus, and Odysseus decides to create a suspenseful tale rather than a straightforward one. It is these narrative decisions that make the so-called special effects in this section so convincing.

By allowing Odysseus to tell these stories in the first-person, rather than narrating them in the third person, Homer draws the reader in and creates a sense of immediacy. He puts us on the scene, giving us the sensation that we are sitting among Odysseus's audience. Instead of regarding the story at arm's length, as we might when reading a third-person narration, we identify with Odysseus's listeners. Like them, we find ourselves leaning forward to hear what will happen next. In addition to luring the audience further into the story, the choice to narrate these books in Odysseus's voice lends urgency and proximity to the events described. Because the character Odysseus actually experienced the adventures he describes, his account of them is more compelling and convincing than a narrator's account would be. When he describes the "sweet transports" he enjoys in Circe's bed, or the "brains and mingled gore" covering the ground of Cyclops's cave, the details—the special effects—are especially vivid because the speaker is not a faceless author but a participant describing what he saw with his own eyes.

In addition to his presence as first-person narrator, it is Odysseus's incredible facility for constructing gripping narratives that makes the individual elements in his stories spring to life. He has a variety of tactics for creating suspense, one of the most effective of which involves forcing the audience to wait for key information.

Instead of giving the headlines first and then filling in the story, as one would when writing a summary of Odysseus's adventures, he sets the scene, hints that something big is going to happen, and then, after prolonging the anticipation, describes the main event. For example, he takes his time setting the scene on Aeaea, describing Circe's lineage, the terrain of the island, and what the men found there to eat. At last, he shares the really fascinating information, the things that his audience actually wants to hear about: what happened when the men were turned into dogs and what it was like being Circe's lover. Odysseus also has a knack for intentionally inspiring unease in his audience. Like a movie director who knows that the sudden appearance of a murderer will be even more terrifying if it is preceded by two minutes of silence, Odysseus understands the value of setting an eerily perfect scene that signals the approach of a disaster. Before he and his men go to Cyclops's cave, for instance, he spends a great deal of time detailing the restful night they passed on the ship, the "pleasing ground" they saw upon awakening, and the "nine fat goats" they killed for food. The idyllic quality of the scene is unsettling, giving us a pleasant thrill of fear in anticipation of what will happen next.

Books 9 through 12 of *The Odyssey* are filled with first-rate special effects: blood and bones, cruel giants, daring escapes, sexually ravenous sorceresses, and more. But carelessly deployed, these same effects could make up the ingredients of a tawdry melodrama. It is the skill with which they are embedded in the narrative that makes them spring off the page in such a compelling fashion.

GLOSSARY OF LITERARY TERMS

ANTAGONIST

> The entity that acts to frustrate the goals of the *protagonist*. The antagonist is usually another *character* but may also be a non-human force.

ANTIHERO / ANTIHEROINE

> A *protagonist* who is not admirable or who challenges notions of what should be considered admirable.

CHARACTER

> A person, animal, or any other thing with a personality that appears in a *narrative*.

CLIMAX

> The moment of greatest intensity in a text or the major turning point in the *plot*.

CONFLICT

> The central struggle that moves the *plot* forward. The conflict can be the *protagonist*'s struggle against fate, nature, society, or another person.

FIRST-PERSON POINT OF VIEW

> A literary style in which the *narrator* tells the story from his or her own *point of view* and refers to himself or herself as "I." The narrator may be an active participant in the story or just an observer.

HERO / HEROINE

> The principal *character* in a literary work or *narrative*.

IMAGERY

> Language that brings to mind sense-impressions, representing things that can be seen, smelled, heard, tasted, or touched.

MOTIF

> A recurring idea, structure, contrast, or device that develops or informs the major *themes* of a work of literature.

NARRATIVE

> A story.

NARRATOR

The person (sometimes a *character*) who tells a story; the *voice* assumed by the writer. The narrator and the author of the work of literature are not the same person.

PLOT

The arrangement of the events in a story, including the sequence in which they are told, the relative emphasis they are given, and the causal connections between events.

POINT OF VIEW

The *perspective* that a *narrative* takes toward the events it describes.

PROTAGONIST

The main *character* around whom the story revolves.

SETTING

The location of a *narrative* in time and space. Setting creates mood or atmosphere.

SUBPLOT

A secondary *plot* that is of less importance to the overall story but may serve as a point of contrast or comparison to the main plot.

SYMBOL

An object, *character,* figure, or color that is used to represent an abstract idea or concept. Unlike an *emblem,* a symbol may have different meanings in different contexts.

SYNTAX

The way the words in a piece of writing are put together to form lines, phrases, or clauses; the basic structure of a piece of writing.

THEME

A fundamental and universal idea explored in a literary work.

TONE

The author's attitude toward the subject or *characters* of a story or poem or toward the reader.

VOICE

An author's individual way of using language to reflect his or her own personality and attitudes. An author communicates voice through *tone, diction,* and *syntax*.

A Note on Plagiarism

Plagiarism—presenting someone else's work as your own—rears its ugly head in many forms. Many students know that copying text without citing it is unacceptable. But some don't realize that even if you're not quoting directly, but instead are paraphrasing or summarizing, *it is plagiarism* unless you cite the source.

Here are the most common forms of plagiarism:

- Using an author's phrases, sentences, or paragraphs without citing the source
- Paraphrasing an author's ideas without citing the source
- Passing off another student's work as your own

How do you steer clear of plagiarism? You should *always* acknowledge all words and ideas that aren't your own by using quotation marks around verbatim text or citations like footnotes and endnotes to note another writer's ideas. For more information on how to give credit when credit is due, ask your teacher for guidance or visit www.sparknotes.com.

REVIEW & RESOURCES

QUIZ

1. In Penelope's archery contest, through how many axes must Odysseus fire his arrow?

    A. two
    B. eight
    C. twelve
    D. thirty

2. Which plant makes the sailors forget their desire to return home?

    A. Lotus
    B. Poppy
    C. Lethe-root
    D. Hemlock

3. How does Athena disguise herself to make preparations for Telemachus's journey?

    A. As a beggar
    B. As Antinous
    C. As Mentor
    D. As Mephistopheles

4. Who is Argos?

    A. The master of the winds
    B. Penelope's chief suitor
    C. The Cyclops
    D. Odysseus's old dog

5. Who first finds Odysseus on the island of Scheria?

    A. Telemachus
    B. King Alcinous
    C. Nausicaa
    D. Circe

87

6. Who has an affair with Eurymachus?

    A. Melantho
    B. Penelope
    C. Circe
    D. Helen

7. Menelaus is king of which city?

    A. Pylos
    B. Argos
    C. Athens
    D. Sparta

8. Eurycleia recognizes Odysseus based on what distinguishing feature?

    A. A scar on his leg
    B. His cunning
    C. The sound of his voice
    D. His "noble bearing"

9. How is Odysseus able to listen safely to the Sirens' song?

    A. He has his men bind him to the ship's mast.
    B. Athena makes the Sirens appear ugly to him.
    C. He eats a lotus flower, rendering him unable to swim to the Sirens' island.
    D. He isn't; he plugs his ears with wax as the ship passes the Sirens' island.

10. Who begs Odysseus to bury him?

    A. Laertes
    B. Polyphemus
    C. Elpenor
    D. Achilles

11. Of what did Odysseus's mother die?

    A. Grief
    B. Drowning
    C. Old age
    D. Starvation

12.   How old is Telemachus at the start of the epic?

    A.   Early thirties
    B.   Early teens
    C.   Early twenties
    D.   Late forties

13.   What happens to the disloyal maids after they clean the blood from the great hall?

    A.   They are hanged.
    B.   They are forgiven.
    C.   They are whipped.
    D.   They are dismissed from the palace.

14.   What does Tiresias warn Odysseus not to harm on his voyage?

    A.   The eagle of the Moon
    B.   The serpent of the Seas
    C.   The cattle of the Sun
    D.   The badger of the Mountains

15.   Who kills Antinous's father?

    A.   Eumaeus
    B.   Odysseus
    C.   Telemachus
    D.   Laertes

16.   In about what year was *The Odyssey* composed?

    A.   C.E. 1590
    B.   700 B.C.E.
    C.   200 B.C.E.
    D.   1200 B.C.E.

17.   Who transforms Odysseus's sailors into pigs?

    A.   Calypso
    B.   Athena
    C.   Poseidon
    D.   Circe

18.   Odysseus left Penelope bound for what city?

    A.   Orinda
    B.   Athens
    C.   Sparta
    D.   Troy

19.   Which goddess often assists Odysseus and Telemachus, and speaks up for them in the councils of the gods on Mount Olympus?

    A.   Calypso
    B.   Athena
    C.   Circe
    D.   Melantho

20.   Why does Poseidon despise Odysseus?

    A.   Odysseus does not respect the sea.
    B.   Odysseus and his men attacked him.
    C.   Odysseus tricked him with a disguise.
    D.   Odysseus blinded his son.

21.   Which two characters provide a point of comparison for Odysseus and Telemachus?

    A.   Athena and Zeus
    B.   Poseidon and Proteus
    C.   Helen and Menelaus
    D.   Agamemnon and Orestes

22.   Who does Zeus send to rescue Odysseus from Calypso?

    A.   Hermes
    B.   Athena
    C.   Poseidon
    D.   Nausicaa

23. What did Ajax do to bring disaster upon the homecoming Greek fleet?

    A. He ate all of the army's remaining rations.
    B. He murdered sheep.
    C. He led the fleet between Scylla and Charybdis.
    D. He raped Cassandra.

24. What gift does Telemachus accept from Menelaus?

    A. A monkey
    B. A chariot and team of horses
    C. A silver mixing-bowl finished with a lip of gold
    D. A band of goats

25. How long does Odysseus spend on Calypso's island?

    A. One year
    B. Seven years
    C. Ten years
    D. Three years

Suggestions for Further Reading

BRANN, EVA. *Homeric Moments: Clues to Delight in Reading* THE ODYSSEY *and* THE ILIAD. Philadelphia: Paul Dry Books, 2002.

BURKERT, WALTER. *Greek Religion.* Translated by John Raffan. Cambridge, MA: Harvard University Press, reprint edition 2006.

CLARKE, HOWARD W. *The Art of* THE ODYSSEY. London: Bristol Classical Press, new edition 1994.

CLAY, JENNY STRAUSS. *The Wrath of Athena: Gods and Men in* THE ODYSSEY. Lanham, MD: Littlefield Adams, 1996.

FINLEY, M. I. *The World of Odysseus.* New York: New York Review Books, reprint edition 2002.

GRIFFIN, JASPER. *Homer:* THE ODYSSEY. Cambridge: Cambridge University Press, reprint edition 2003.

KIRK, G. S. *The Songs of Homer.* Cambridge: Cambridge University Press, new edition 2004.

KNOX, BERNARD. "Introduction." In Homer, *The Odyssey*, trans. Robert Fagles. New York: Penguin Books, 1996.

LOUDEN, BRUCE. THE ODYSSEY: *Structure, Narration, and Meaning.* Baltimore, MD: Johns Hopkins University Press, 2001.

NAGY, GREGORY. *The Best of the Achaeans: Concepts of the Hero in Archaic Greek Poetry.* Baltimore: Johns Hopkins University Press, revised edition 1998.

PAGE, DENYS. *The Homeric* ODYSSEY. Westport, CT: Greenwood Publishing Group, Inc., 1982.